Hill and Rae shrewdly reveal the positive effects of re~~___~~ on economic performance. Even in the midst of the ~~___~~ show that capitalism in the United States is shaped ~~___~~ man economically more and morally better than a mere "naked individual who was the sum of his individual appetites." Like Adam Smith before them, Hill and Rae rightly return moral sentiment to what makes for the wealth of nations. This vital message couldn't come at a more propitious moment—as a needed guide to Americans as we begin to work our way back to a morally founded prosperity.

—TONY BLANKLEY, columnist, *The Washington Times*

Freedom flourishes when individuals can succeed and see their entrepreneurial dreams turn into reality. Capitalism deserves the credit. *The Virtues of Capitalism*'s examination of the importance of this foundation of the free market is a unique approach. The authors make a biblical and moral correlation, while explaining and discrediting recent attacks against a free society. Fans and skeptics alike will find a compelling read.

—U.S. Congressman JOHN SHADEGG, Arizona

Now, more than ever, the "moral case for free markets" needs to be heard loudly and clearly. Not only do our broader liberties hinge on economic freedom, but our nonnegotiable duty to help the poor depends on a robust market economy understood within a moral framework. With *The Virtues of Capitalism*, Austin Hill and Scott Rae have made a compelling and compassionate case.

—THE REV. ROBERT A. SIRICO, president and cofounder of
the Acton Institute for the Study of Religion and Liberty,
and author of *The Entrepreneurial Vocation*

Capitalism has taken a beating in the popular press over the past few years, and that's a shame. Done right, capitalism captures the spirit of America by rewarding the diligent for their hard work and challenging the lazy to work harder. *The Virtues of Capitalism* takes an honest look at the system, celebrating its strengths and spotlighting its weaknesses. This should be required reading in every college in the country!

—DAVE RAMSEY, host of *The Dave Ramsey Show*
and bestselling author of *The Total Money Makeover*

Everyone knows that free markets are more efficient than command-and-control economies where the government runs everything. But Austin Hill and Scott Rae make the important and persuasive case that capitalism is also more fair, more decent, more moral than any system that hands control to bureaucrats and politicians. They have made a valuable contribution to the most significant contemporary debates.

—MICHAEL MEDVED, nationally syndicated talk show host
and author of *The 5 Big Lies about American Business*

Now that our Great Recession has given new hope to those who would toss out the engine of economic progress, *The Virtues of Capitalism* is especially timely. Hill and Rae readably and persuasively show how biblical wisdom and human experience both support free markets. Professors, students, and general readers looking for an alternative to propaganda should buy and read this book.

—DR. MARVIN OLASKY, provost of The King's College, New York City,
and editor-in-chief of *World* magazine

Austin Hill and Dr. Scott Rae follow in the footsteps of some of history's most profound philosophers in drawing the essential connection between freedom and that which is objectively good. From Adam Smith to Frederic Bastiat to Ludwig von Mises to Milton Friedman, some of our greatest minds have reached the inevitable conclusion that capitalism—for all its perceived faults—is our most morally correct and virtuous form of social organization. I applaud Austin and Scott for reinterpreting that truth for a new age and a new generation.

—GOVERNOR BUTCH OTTER, Idaho

A fascinating read about the moral and ethical implications of our economic systems. Drawing a clear distinction between self interest and "greed," *The Virtues Of Capitalism* takes us to the very heart of who we are and the nature of our worldly pursuits.

—GEOFF CURRIER, talk show host, 680 CJOB Radio, Winnipeg, Manitoba

Every community—indeed every country—needs creative business people who work hard and follow the rules. Whether it's the inventor, small business operator, franchisee, or corporate executive, we're all reliant on the willingness of business professionals to take risks with their time, talents, and money so as to create better products and services and, thus, employment opportunities that benefit the entire community. In *The Virtues Of Capitalism*, Austin Hill and Scott Rae have explained why our economic system must provide an environment of respect for worthy business people, and encourage this kind of creativity and healthy risk-taking. It is a must-read for anyone who cares about the future of our economy and our country.

—MATT MCMAHON, Outback Steakhouse Restaurants

For its people to truly be free and prosperous, every society requires an economic system that both cares for and empowers its weakest members, while respecting its wealth creators. President Ronald Reagan made the political case for that structure. In *The Virtues of Capitalism*, Austin Hill and Scott Rae provide the moral basis for such a society.

—HUGH HALLMAN, JD; mayor of Tempe, Arizona, and
cofounder of the Kazakh-American Free University in Kazakhstan

As expected, Austin Hill and Scott Rae knock it out of the park. *The Virtues Of Capitalism* is an overdue contribution to the great debate of our time and reminds us of what our country ought to look like. Hill and Rae are second to none in laying out the case for capitalism, individualism, and in the final analysis, for America itself.

—CHRIS PLANTE, talk show host, 630 WMAL Radio, Washington, D.C.

Part history, part economics, part philosophy, and part contemporary events, *The Virtues of Capitalism* forces one to think deeply about both economics and personal values.

—DR. RICHARD RAWLS, associate professor of history,
Georgia Gwinnett College

The

VIRTUES

of

CAPITALISM

A Moral Case for Free Markets

AUSTIN HILL AND SCOTT RAE

NORTHFIELD PUBLISHING
CHICAGO

Editor: Jim Vincent
Interior Design: Smartt Guys design
Cover Design and Image: Tan Nguyen

Library of Congress Cataloging-in-Publication Data

Hill, Austin, 1964-
    The virtues of capitalism : a moral case for free markers / Austin Hill and Scott Rae.
        p. cm.
    Includes bibliographical references.
    ISBN 978-0-8024-8456-7
    1. Capitalism—Moral and ethical aspects. 2. Capitalism—Religious aspects.
    3. Economic policy. I. Rae, Scott B. II. Title.
    HB501.H516 2010
    174—dc22

                                                                    2010001954

We hope you enjoy this book from Northfield Publishing. Our goal is to provide high-quality, thought-provoking books and products that connect truth to your real needs and challenges. For more information on other books and products written and produced from a biblical perspective, go to www.moodypublishers.com or write to:

Northfield Publishing
820 North LaSalle Boulevard
Chicago, IL 60610

1 3 5 7 9 10 8 6 4 2

Printed in the United States of America

To Nell Dunivent Hill, my wife.
Thank you for believing.
To Graham, my son.
May the ideas in this book help to shape your world.

To my late father, Walter B. Rae,
who modeled the character traits we discuss
and whose business illustrated the virtues of capitalism.

CONTENTS

Economics: A social science concerned chiefly with description and analysis of the production, distribution, and consumption of goods and services.

—MERRIAM-WEBSTER'S COLLEGIATE DICTIONARY, ELEVENTH EDITION

1

"I ONLY CARE
about the
MORAL ISSUES"

Can somebody name for me one area of our lives that has nothing to do with economics?"

With this question, a hush fell upon the room inside the retreat center. For a moment the only thing to be heard was the sound of a babbling brook traveling through the open window—a very common sound for rural northwestern Connecticut in the summertime. The speaker, an economist from Auburn University, had just finished leading the group of thirty or so graduate students in a "let's go around the room and introduce ourselves" exercise and was now homing in on what would be a central topic for the meeting.

It was the summer of 1996. I (Austin) was one of those graduate students —from across the United States and Canada, and from among multiple academic fields—who had been invited to gather at this private, low-key event with some writers and university professors, to discuss the rather abstract concept of "human liberty." I was excited to be at the conference and was eager to learn. But I had no idea where this little three-day weekend was going to lead.

I was silently contemplating an answer to the professor's question, *Was there any area of my life that had nothing to do with economics?* when a student named Hubbard spoke up.

Hubbard had just introduced himself to the group moments before, as we all had done. He had explained that he was working toward a master's degree at a theological seminary in Louisville, Kentucky. And while he had indicated that his first name was indeed Hubbard, he had also successfully moved the entire group past the awkwardness of being in a room full of strangers, and had even gotten us all to smile and laugh and applaud for him just a bit, when he told us in his charming Southern accent, "Y'all can just call me Hub." And now Hub was answering the first, big, deep question of the day.

"As a Christian," he said looking at the professor, "I believe that my eternal salvation has nothing to do with economics."

"Okay," the professor responded. "Let's assume that you're right about that, Hub. And let's assume that what is true for Hub is true for everyone; that there is, indeed, an 'afterlife,' and that one's ultimate destination in the afterlife has nothing to do with economics. Now, having said that, can somebody name for me a second area of our lives that has nothing to do with economics?" The room got real quiet again. "My friends," the professor said after several seconds of dead silence, "let me suggest to you that there is no other area of our existence that has nothing to do with economics. Every facet of our earthly lives is impacted on some level by both economic activity, and economic conditions."

Thus began a three-day "seminar" several years ago, when a handful of graduate students gathered together to talk about some weighty ideas. That weekend, and the question that kicked off that weekend, are at least partly responsible for your authors collaborating several years later and producing the book that you're reading right now.

So how would you answer the professor's question? Do you agree with his conclusion? Have you ever been asked this question, or contemplated it yourself? Can you specify an area of your life that is *not* impacted in any way by economics—the production, distribution, and consumption of goods and services? Or do you believe that certain elements of your existence are simply going to be what they're going to be—either by the twist of fate, or by your own choosing, or by the hand of God, or a combination of all three—and economic conditions simply don't change anything?

Most people would agree that, in a broad sense, economic conditions matter profoundly. They can impact the destiny of nations, the presence and duration of peace, the outcomes of wars, the relative stability of societies, and the well-being of future generations. But when it comes to questions about how economics can impact the private aspects of our lives, the answers are frequently not so obvious. Can the issue of economics influence one's commitments to a spouse, or to children, or to other family members? Does the issue impact the way a person functions in their community, or how one serves the less fortunate?

Some people are troubled by the suggestion that economic conditions can impact their role as a husband, wife, mom, or dad. But be honest and ask yourself: Is it ever more difficult to be the kind of spouse or parent that one aspires to be, when the economy is slow and personal finances are scarce? And—here's a tough one—when finances are plentiful, can the enjoyment of material goods enable a person to avoid or neglect other important areas of their relationships? And a final question, one some people find even more difficult to ponder: Can economics impact one's relationship with their God?

We respect the point that Hub made about his Christian faith and the issue of eternal salvation. But we also realize that there is more to a person's spiritual life than his or her eternal destiny. Life on this side of eternity matters as well, and economics has a great deal to do with life on this side. It's interesting to note that in the Bible, Jesus Himself had far more to say about money and economics than He did about eternity.

To this end, we think it's worthwhile to consider how living in either an environment of scarcity or plenty, or under one economic system or another, can impact one's faith in a benevolent, all-good God.

Just as the economist said to the students at the conference, we believe that *"every facet of our earthly lives is impacted on some level by both economic activity, and economic conditions."* The economy affects individuals and families and entire societies, and it affects both the way a person engages in the world around them, as well as a person's private life.

But what are we to make of the morality of economics? Should economics be regarded as a "moral issue" at all? Economic systems and policies are, in part, an expression of how a society regards both its weakest and most powerful members, and all those in between; they often play a key role in determining who "wins" and who "loses" in a society; and they can both encourage and discourage positive, productive behavior among the citizenry. Over the course of history, some societies have chosen economic systems that have helped a large percentage of its citizens to enjoy social and economic success. Other societies have utilized economic systems that have caused the few to flourish while the many were trampled upon.

Although this book is about the philosophical and moral underpinnings of capitalism, we also must acknowledge that capitalism itself, as well as other types of economic systems, is enabled in part by certain types of governmental and political structures. And while we are not writing about politics, per se, we nonetheless need to discuss to some degree the types of political structures and environments that have been necessary for the various types of economic systems to exist. We'll do this in more detail in chapter 8. For now we acknowledge that economics, much like politics, requires us to answer the question *"How shall we order our lives together?"* This question is, fundamentally, a moral one. And for this reason, it is perplexing that one of the most influential political movements in recent history—a movement that by its own definition has been devoted to bringing "moral issues" to light in American politics—has had very little to say, if anything, about economics. This is the faith-based-voters movement, and we will examine its social and political involvement during the past three decades.

SO WHAT ARE THE "MORAL ISSUES" AND WHO IS FOCUSED ON THEM?

Regardless of their political leanings, whether liberal or conservative, left-leaning or right-leaning, a huge number of Americans identify their "core moral convictions" as the chief motivator for them to let their voices be heard in American politics. Perhaps you would say this about yourself as well. Often those moral convictions are derived from their commitments to a faith tradition, and they are most compelled to participate in the American political process when certain moral issues—usually a select few issues having to do with their core values—are weighing in the balance.

To be clear, we are not assuming here that all religious Americans are seeking to advance their personal "moral values" in the public arena. We recognize that there have always been some Americans who argue that moral beliefs are inherently private matters, and that these matters don't belong in policy debates. Similarly, we are aware that at present a growing number of Americans —many of them religious—are becoming increasingly disillusioned with the idea of voicing their moral concerns in the political arena. We respect those who view moral issues in this way, although we maintain that public policy entails moral concerns—and ultimately, public policy impacts everyone.

Having said that, we recognize that many Americans care deeply about the moral aspects of public policy, are informed and motivated by their faith, and desire that their voices be heard in the political process. One of the largest and most influential of these categories is what we will be referring to as faith-based individuals and groups. We focus on them because we know them well and they are a good example of the point we are making in this chapter, not because they are the only group who cares about public morality.

According to research from the Pew Forum on Religion and Public Life, 70 percent of American adults identify with evangelical Protestant Christianity, "mainline denominational" Protestant Christianity, Catholicism, Orthodox Judaism, or Mormonism. Since many members of these religious groups share common, strongly held beliefs and values, it is not surprising that over the past several decades they have often exhibited similar responses to public policy concerns amid America's changing cultural landscape.[1] Again, we are not suggesting that they are the only people among the American electorate with a moral conscience, or who vote according to their core moral convictions. Obviously, many Americans regard voting in our nation's elections as both a responsibility and a privilege, and their moral convictions play a profound part in the selections they make on a ballot. Additionally, people of great faith, good intentions, and moral conviction reside on both the conservative political right and on the liberal political left, and at varying times and in varying proportions they have aligned with both the Democratic and Republican political parties. Our focus on faith-based voters is simply one effective example to illustrate our perplexity that economics is not widely regarded as a moral issue.

From our observations, faith-based voters have by their own definition focused almost exclusively on a few key moral issues confronting our nation, while at times ignoring other public policy concerns that they do not perceive as moral issues. And this is the central dilemma that we are getting at: Because economics has not been adequately defined as a "moral issue" by these faith-based groups, far too many faith-based voters have too often ignored economic issues. In other instances, they have been ambivalent about the various choices that confront them in the arena of economic policy.

We remain intrigued with the influence of the faith-based voters movement and its ability to motivate people to action over their concern for moral issues. In a moment we'll consider where this movement may be heading, and why economics and an accurate view of capitalism need to be at the movement's center. But first let's consider how this focus on "moral issues" among faith-based voters got started in the first place.

THE EARLY YEARS

Since the time of America's founding, moral questioning, reasoning, and argumentation have remained a part of the nation's public policy debates. Not only that, but moral dialogue has also been at the epicenter of some of our nation's biggest public policy developments. The eradication of slavery, the emergence of the New Deal, the civil rights movement, and the nation's engagement in the Vietnam War all come to mind; at times, this dialogue has entailed explicitly religious tones and themes. As such, the reality of moral and religious ideas impacting our government is not new.

The beginnings of what we know today as the modern faith-based political movement can be traced back to the late 1960s. After having been quite disengaged from politics for a number of years, and without much in the way of formal organization, millions of American Christians—at that time mostly white, middle-class, Protestant and evangelical Christians—were becoming increasingly alarmed at the current-day cultural trends and growing civil unrest of the late 1960s and early 1970s.

The challenges to marriage and Judeo-Christian sexual norms posed by the so-called "sexual revolution"; the youthful rebellion against societal authority structures brought about by the growing "hippie" culture; and the Vietnam War protests by many American youth who thought it was something less than "honorable" to fight on behalf of the country—all these developments proved to be sufficiently unnerving to these millions of Americans.

In the midst of this cultural upheaval U.S. President Richard Nixon delivered an important address to the nation on November 3, 1969. During the address, Nixon made reference to a so-called silent majority of Americans—people who supposedly agreed with him on issues of culture, "law and order," and the war, even though their views of such things may largely have gone unnoticed. In using the "silent majority" phrase, Nixon sought to awaken politically this large number of Americans who did not participate in public discourse, who did not have a voice in American media, who often did not vote, and who did not publicly "demonstrate" on behalf of causes they believed in. Yet this sector of American society was nonetheless very real and very frustrated by what they believed was a degradation of America and its institutions.

Some people believed that the use of the "silent majority" phrase was nothing more than the president "playing politics" and creating a theme for his re-election campaign (and doing so very early in his first term). Others took offense to the terminology, claiming that with the phrase "silent majority," the president was dismissing the "voices of dissent"—the "vocal minority," if you will—who dared to speak out against their government and oppose the Vietnam War.

But regardless of how the president's words were interpreted at the time, there's no disputing that Nixon's efforts to reach out to the "silent majority" in a time of cultural chaos changed the electoral dynamics in America. And three years after uttering those words for the first time and introducing the theme of the silent majority (combined with another three years of war protests and social upheaval), Nixon won the hearts and minds of a majority of both Republicans and Democrats with a forty-nine-state electoral college landslide in the 1972 presidential election.

FROM "SILENT MAJORITY" TO "MORAL MAJORITY" TO THE WHITE HOUSE

Nixon began his second term as president on January 20, 1973, although he would only last in office another nineteen months. In August 1974 he became the only U.S. president to resign from office, when faced with the near certainty of impeachment for his role in the Watergate scandal. Still, the cultural upheaval of the time, and Nixon's response to it, had politically awakened a portion of the American population in a way that would mark American politics for decades to come, and that would eventually give rise to what we think of today as faith-based voters.

The formation of this new political force actually was further strengthened two days after Nixon's second term began. On January 22, 1973, the United States Supreme Court rendered its now famous *Roe v. Wade* decision, which determined that a mother may abort the life of her child in the womb for any reason, up until the "point at which the fetus becomes 'viable.'" As to what was meant by "viable," the court defined this as "potentially able to live outside the mother's womb, albeit with artificial aid." While four years earlier it seemed to many that America and its institutions were being degraded, now it appeared to many that the very definition of human life itself was also being compromised.

Over the next few years, many Americans began to view the United States as a nation in moral decline as a president had resigned his office, South Vietnam was lost, the beginning of human life was called into question by the Supreme Court, and the value of marriage was being downplayed by the now-blossoming feminist movement.

The 1976 election of Jimmy Carter as president marked a bit of a turning point for the many Americans who were distraught over the nation's course. This was especially true for the nation's many evangelical Christians, as Carter himself was the first self-professed evangelical to ascend to the office. Carter, a Democrat, appealed to many faith-based voters, and his election symbolized the tremendous political power that could be wielded by people of faith traditions who shared similar cultural views, when, in fact, they actually voted. During Carter's presidency this faith-based political influence became more officially organized, with the founding of the groups Christian Voice, Sojourners, and later the Moral Majority.

THE REPUBLICAN APPEAL
TO THE FAITH COMMUNITY

Similarly, it was no surprise when, in the face of Carter's election, and the growing political influence of faith-based voters, the Republican party made a powerful appeal for their votes. Challenging President Carter in the 1980 election, Ronald Reagan successfully swayed a majority of faith-based groups and individuals to the "right" side of the political aisle, with both a pledged commitment to "moral values," yet also with a promise of a stronger, more robust foreign policy, and greater American influence around the world, as well.

During the course of Reagan's two-term presidency, and the one term of President George H. W. Bush, religious faith-based advocacy groups sprang up in significant number, most (but not all) of which leaned to the political right. The groundbreaking Moral Majority organization officially folded in 1989, but other groups like the Family Research Council, the Christian Coalition, Concerned Women for America, and Focus on the Family hit their stride, finding large audiences and gaining tremendous political influence. Not surprisingly, given the beginnings of this movement during the social upheaval of the Nixon era, groups of this sort that "leaned right" got in the habit of collectively referring to themselves as being a part of the "pro-family movement," and identified abortion, poverty, parental rights, children's sex education, combating pornography, and the definition of marriage as moral issues. At the same time, groups that tended more toward the political left, such as the Sojourners and other groups emerging from mainline denominations, arose in part to challenge the view of morality expressed by what has been known as the religious right.

THE "MORAL ISSUE" BEGGING FOR ATTENTION

Today, many faith-based individuals and groups face dramatic new challenges amid America's changing cultural and political landscape. They have added embryonic stem cell research and the definition of marriage as subjects worthy of the care and attention of America's faith-based voters and extended the issue of the value of the unborn. On these final two issues (definition of marriage and the sanctity of life in the womb), President Barack Obama and members of his administration seemingly take an opposing viewpoint at nearly every turn. Yet, with respect to other important moral issues, including caring for the poor, availability of health care, and protection of the environment, left-leaning faith-based voters may feel as though this current era is one of tremendous opportunity and advancement.

In the midst of the current public policy landscape, the response from both left-leaning and right-leaning Americans who purport to care about the moral issues lacks substantive thought on domestic economic issues. For example, faith-based Americans on the "right" continue to articulate their moral concerns about life in the womb, parental rights, and the definition of marriage. Yet, they have been criticized for ignoring the needs of the poor, and for paying no attention to the need to properly care for the environment—and both of these issues have much to do with economics.

Meanwhile, faith-based Americans on the left frequently seem pleased with the government's plans for universal health care, mortgage retention assistance, "green energy" strategies, environmental protections, and universal college education. They applaud policy efforts on immigration, health care, and education in terms of "caring for the poor," and describe governmental efforts toward environmental protection in terms that are reflective of the story of creation in the book of Genesis. Yet these Americans rarely express the same level of moral concern over the staggering levels of debt that the U.S. federal government is accruing as a result of some of these new initiatives, and they seem to be lacking concern over the increasing entanglement of government with private business, and the loss of personal freedom that ensues from such entanglements.

Thus, while faith-based groups and individuals remain mostly silent on the moral issues of economics, moral reflections on economic policy instead emanate from distinctly nonreligious groups and institutions.[2] For example, most moral critiques of economic globalization are entirely secular in nature, and most reflect negatively on the phenomenon of globalization.

We were impressed by a particular example of a secular institution offering a moral critique of the economy while faith-based groups remained silent. It happened to be the same week that a "G20 Summit" was underway in London. During that week in March 2009 the *London Telegraph* newspaper published a striking editorial entitled "G20 Summit Must Make the Moral Case for Capitalism." The editorial and the summit itself should have been a kind of "call to arms" for those who care about capitalism, and the morality of economic policy generally. Yet the *Telegraph* editorial seemed to provide a "lone voice" amid most of the reporting and editorializing on the summit.

As a radio talk show host and columnist, I (Austin) covered the last presidential campaign cycle, and the historic election of Barack Obama, in tremendous detail. I watched and listened as Republican John McCain sought to blame the October 2008 stock market crash entirely on "corporate greed," and as Democrat Barack Obama promised to raise taxes on "rich Americans" and give all "the rest of us" a tax cut. I also frequently spoke with callers to my talk shows, many of whom wanted to talk about the candidates' stances on abortion, the environment, the definition of marriage, and health-care distribution. With these callers, I would often try to probe economic questions, asking things like, "Do you think Senator Obama's plan to raise taxes on wealthier Americans is fair?" or "Do you think John McCain is right? Is the downturn all because of greed on Wall Street?" Over and over, I received essentially the same response to my question: "I only care about the moral issues"—as though the economic issues were morally neutral, or of little moral significance.

America is now in the midst of an economic policy revolution. Faith-based individuals and groups can no longer afford to sit on the sidelines and pretend that economics is *not* a moral issue. Nor can they assume that the various economic systems in the world are all morally equivalent with one another. Given the severe mismanagement of private sector financial markets, and the global economic turmoil and the loss of confidence in American-styled capitalism that has resulted, the need for sound, moral understanding of the economy is as great as it ever has been.

CHARTING THE COURSE

Despite its flaws, failures, and imperfections, capitalism remains the most moral choice among the world's economic systems. Not only do we believe that it is the preferred choice, we also believe that capitalism is most consistent with a Judeo-Christian view of the world. It also best honors the human person, and is the way in which we can most productively order our lives together. So beginning in chapter 2, we'll take a look at what the Judeo-Christian tradition—mostly through the lens of the Bible—has to say about economics, and demonstrate the consistencies between the Bible and capitalist principles.

Let's chart the course for the other chapters as well. In chapter 3, "Ancient Virtues in the Modern Marketplace," we'll look at how capitalism both requires and helps to sustain essential types of moral goodness and virtue. We'll take a brief look at what the world was like before modern capitalism, and then consider how capitalism has improved the human condition. But we'll also see that, while capitalism contributes to our collective reservoir of virtues and moral goodness, it also requires that we all choose to behave virtuously in order for it to be sustained.

Of course, we live in an era of growing doubts about capitalism. So in chapter 4 we'll take on some of the most common criticisms of capitalism. We freely admit that capitalism is far from perfect and will examine some of the negative claims made about it—that it is "based on greed," it instigates "materialism" and "consumerism," and so forth. We'll provide an honest and thorough response to each of them. As we will demonstrate, some of the criticisms are valid. Yet some other criticisms are based on faulty assumptions about economics, or in some cases, faulty assumptions about Judeo-Christian teaching, and about ethics, generally.

In chapter 5, we'll ponder the question "Did Capitalism Fail?" Given the hardship that resulted from the "Great Recession" of the early twenty-first century, many people claim that capitalism has failed, and still others say that capitalism is an idea whose time has come and gone. But as we'll see, capitalism has not failed; the global financial system did, but not capitalism as a whole. We'll further argue that at least some of the causes of the late 2000s' downturn had to do with government, not capitalism. That is, unintended consequences of government intervention in the market along with short-sighted public policy created the conditions in which greed flourished.

From there, we'll examine the ongoing shift in economic public policy that is underway in America as a response to the recent recession. In chapter 6, we'll make the case that the desire for more government controls over the economy is understandable, but not necessarily helpful. We'll also demonstrate how some of government's best attempts to "fix" financial problems actually exacerbate them.

In chapter 7, we'll address "Corporate Greed and the Politics of Envy." In this chapter, we'll demonstrate how genuine greed seems to have brought down the financial sector. We'll also see how this bad behavior often begets really bad public policy from politicians and policy makers who are, quite naturally, eager to intervene in the private economy and attempt to "help."

Finally, we'll examine the limits on the market. Chapter 8 reminds us capitalism can't do it all. While we believe that capitalism has the ability to transform individual lives, communities, and nations, we recognize that there is a role to be played by religious institutions, nonprofit groups, and governments in building a cohesive society. We will also detail how capitalism must be guided by a "moral-cultural system" in order for its participants to continue flourishing and to remain prosperous.

So is economics a moral issue? Join us as we consider why that is so, and how capitalism, properly understood, is consistent with both the Bible and some very important and widely held virtues.

NOTES

1. "U.S. Religious Landscape Survey," 2009, The Pew Forum on Religion and Public Life, Washington, D.C., http://religions.pewforum.org/reports.
2. One notable exception is the work of Sojourners founder Jim Wallis. See his recent work, *Rediscovering Values: A Moral Compass for the New Economy* (New York: Howard, 2010).

I think that we have failed them in our churches, our schools and our government. And I certainly think the free market has failed. We've all failed.[1]

—THEN-SENATOR HILLARY CLINTON, SPEAKING ABOUT AMERICA'S
YOUTH AT A FAITH AND VALUES FORUM

THE BIBLE

on

ECONOMICS

The Bible and economics. Does that seem to you like an odd combination? You might be wondering why we would look to the Bible in the context of a book about capitalism. Further, you may doubt that such an ancient book could possibly have anything to say about our modern, global, information-based economy. But there is good reason to look to the Bible in a book about capitalism.

For centuries, philosophers, economists, and theologians have reflected on the intersection of ethics and economics. Many theological works, and the teachings of Jesus Himself, tackle economics and can inform our view of economic *systems*. Interestingly, many of the theologians who have commented on economics through the centuries have taken a dim view of commerce and business.

Of course, for a Christian or someone who sees life from a Judeo-Christian worldview, the Bible is the first resource to consult. Even if you are not a religious person, it makes sense to take a good look at what the Bible says. This is because most people, even those who are not particularly religious, see the

Bible as a helpful guide in matters of morality. For example, the Ten Commandments and the Sermon on the Mount are widely viewed as some of the most insightful material around on matters of morality. More specifically, for centuries, cultures have looked to the Bible as a rich resource that has helped people think about the way morality and economics come together. And you might actually be surprised at the wisdom you'll find, and how relevant the Bible still is.

It is true that, when it comes to economics, the world of the Bible and today's global information economy are totally different.[2] In the world of the Bible, most people made their living from the land—in agriculture, or in a modest trade (such as Jesus' carpentry business or His disciples' fishing business). It was often difficult to get ahead financially—most people would remain in the socioeconomic station of life into which they were born. Historian D. E. Oakman insists that "for the majority of the population, after they had paid their taxes, there was barely enough to eat."[3] There were few "rags to riches" stories in the ancient world. Most of the rich became wealthy through inheritance, patronage, or corruption, sometimes by abusing political power (like the tax collectors) or exploiting the vulnerable. One of the reasons the Old Testament prophets condemned the rich, beyond the obvious temptation of idolatry, was that becoming wealthy often involved oppressing the vulnerable, clearly an immoral means of acquiring wealth.

But that's not all that was different. In the ancient world, no one except the very rich retired—most people simply worked until they were unable to work any longer. At that point, they relied on their extended family to take care of them. In addition, there was not much saving or investing for the long term, since most goods were perishable[4] (and since there was nothing like today's stock market or other investment vehicles).

Further, the lot of the poor was very difficult, since public assistance, or welfare, from the state didn't really exist, at least not anything like it does today. The poor survived largely on private charity, which meant they were in a precarious financial position. And the poor in the ancient world probably have more in common with the desperately poor in the developing world today than the poor in the West.

Finally, there is a big difference between the global economy of today and the local economy of the ancient world. In biblical times, there was some modest international trade, but most economic activity took place in the local community. There was nothing resembling the global supply chain or the worldwide customer base that many companies have today.

Despite these differences, one key fact about the Bible makes it relevant to this book's aim. The Bible treats economics as a moral issue. It is full of stories and commands that have a lot to do with economics. Though Jesus had little to say about economic systems, He had a lot to say about economic life—about wealth, possessions, and personal morality—but a lot less about economic systems. One way to think about the Bible's contribution to our view of economics is to start from the beginning and follow the path of the Bible as it progressively unfolds its teaching. It's an approach called "biblical theology."

GENESIS:
"IN THE BEGINNING . . ."

Right at the start of the Bible, in the book of Genesis, we learn that God created the world and called it good, making the material world fundamentally good (Genesis 1:31). He further entrusted human beings with dominion over the earth—giving them not only the *privilege* of enjoying the benefits of the material world, but also the *responsibility* for caring for the world, known as the "dominion mandate."[5] From the beginning, God gave human beings the ability to acquire knowledge, accomplish complex tasks, and apply this knowledge for their benefit; this seems clear from the account of human beings naming the animals.[6] In the creation, God exemplified, among other traits, wisdom, intelligence, creativity, and initiative. As a part of what it means for every human being to be made in His image,[7] God set human beings free to utilize their divinely endowed traits. This is all a part of the responsible exercise of dominion over creation that brings innovation and productivity to benefit humankind.

British economist Sir Brian Griffiths rightly sees in the dominion mandate that "man has been created with an urge to control and harness the resources of nature in the interests of the common good, but he is subject to his accountability to God as a trustee to preserve and care for it. This process is precisely what an economist would refer to as *responsible wealth creation*."[8] The dominion mandate coincides with human beings being made in God's image, giving them an innate inclination to utilize the created world for productive purposes.

In the Bible's account of creation, God Himself is portrayed as a worker,[9] who continues working to sustain His world. His creativity, initiative, and resourcefulness displayed in creation are also traits that have been given to human beings by virtue of being made in His image. Though human beings are clearly more than autonomous economic agents, responsible human dominion over creation involves exercising these creative qualities. In Genesis, God also ordained work as a good thing and one of the primary means by which dominion was accomplished (Genesis 2:15), though as a result of the entrance of sin into the world, work was corrupted and made more difficult.[10]

THE OLD TESTAMENT LAW

Economics is a major theme in Old Testament law. In this section of Scripture, Israel becomes a nation "under God" and received a set of guidelines resembling a constitution. Many of these guidelines in the Old Testament law regulate financial dealings. The purpose of Israel's "constitution" was to show how God's people could model His righteousness in the way they lived together as a nation; that is, how they could become a "holy nation."[11]

When it came to economics, there were two main ways that they would do this. One was to make sure that their society was fair—that when people made exchanges, they did so without engaging in fraud or cheating each other. For example, the law mandated that the scales that would weigh out measures of goods were accurate, so that when someone bought a "pound" of something, they could be sure they got a pound's worth.[12] The law assumed that individuals could legitimately own and accumulate property and belongings, since laws prohibiting theft and fraud only make sense if there is something like private property that is accepted. But the law also made it clear that God is the ultimate owner of everything.[13] These two notions are not inconsistent. The Bible affirms that God owns it all and that private owners are caretakers or tenants of His creation. God's essential ownership does not call for a radical redistribution of income, but it does obligate private owners to hold their possessions loosely.

The second way God's people would be a "holy nation" in economics was to ensure that the poor were cared for properly.[14] It was assumed that people were responsible for taking care of themselves and their families, and from there, the focus in the OT law was on how to provide for those who could not provide for themselves. This distinction between capability and incapability provided the very definition of "the poor." In chapter 6 we'll see how some modern-day economic policy doesn't expect capable individuals to take care of themselves, and in some cases shouldn't even be held responsible for their own choices, a striking contrast to this historic Judeo-Christian teaching.

> **The law was concerned about both the overall goals of economic life and the means to accomplish those goals.**

The OT law structured many aspects of economic life to see to it that the poor were not without opportunity to take care of themselves. For example, the law mandated a tradition known as "gleaning," which permitted the poor to make their way through another's agricultural field and gather some of the produce for themselves. The law also provided for a right of redemption of property, so that the poor, who had met misfortune, could have renewed opportunity to make a living themselves.[15] Finally there was the tradition of the year of Jubilee, which returned land to its original owner every fiftieth year.[16]

Consider the tremendous insight of these Old Testament teachings. In ancient Israel, precautions were taken to care for those who truly could not care for themselves. Yet at the same time efforts were made to encourage the poor to care for themselves when they were truly able to do so. This is to say that in the ancient wisdom of the Judeo-Christian tradition, the poor were still encouraged to participate in their own care and provision, even as they received assistance from the community. We'll see in chapter 3 how capitalism is consistent with this wisdom, and later how some current-day economic policy works counter to this wisdom (chapter 6).

The Old Testament law also set forth the Sabbath tradition, which went back to the original creation account, and that mandated a regular day of rest from work. The Sabbath was a sign of God's covenant with the people. One of the main purposes for this was to help the people trust God to provide for them through their six days/week of work. The Sabbath was required even during the harvest and planting times, the busiest and most important times of the year.[17] This is amplified by the provision for the sabbatical year, in which the land was to lie unharvested one year in seven. The people were to trust God to provide for them in the sixth year all they would need for the sabbatical year as well. It seems that the law was concerned both about the overall goals of economic life—to provide for fair dealings and take care of the poor—and the means to accomplish those goals, with such laws as gleaning, redemption, and Jubilee.

Naturally, literally following some of the OT law mandates for economic life in a modern, information-age economy would be pretty difficult. For example, applying the year of Jubilee today would cause considerable upheaval in the real estate business. Further, how could the practice of gleaning work, since so little of the land today is used for agriculture and the economy is not driven by food production?

The differences between economic life in biblical times and today suggest that many of the mandates governing economics in the Bible cannot be applied directly. Rather, the way to use the OT law is to try to discern the general moral principle(s) underlying the specific command, and then look to apply those to the specific situations and institutions we face today.[18] For example, the law of gleaning could be understood to require that the productive people in the society set aside some of their resources to assist the poor (while also requiring that the poor be involved and not simply receive a handout). Or the year of Jubilee might be understood to require that no one be cut off from the opportunity to make a living for themselves, since land was the principal productive asset in the ancient world.[19]

So there are what we might call *cultural* limits on how specifically the OT law can be applied. But a further limit on the use of the OT law is a *hermeneu-*

tical one. That is, much of the OT law is not meant to be directly applied by us today—it was directly applicable only to OT Israel.

To be sure, Israel was to model a society in which economic dealings were fair and the poor were cared for. But the means prescribed to accomplish that are not necessarily the same means for today. The reason is that in the Old Testament, Israel functioned as a *theocracy*, in which the law of God was the law of the land. OT Israel was the only nation in biblical history to be literally "one nation under God," where God's laws were automatically the law of the land.

Of course, some Islamic countries that are under sharia law today would also be theocracies. But the Bible is clear that from New Testament times forward, there is no longer a theocracy—today, God uses the multinational, multiethnic body called the church as the primary agent through which He works out His purposes.

However, all the OT law is profitable for today in its general principles, which are just as important but applicable in different ways that correspond to economic life today.

WISDOM OF THE WISDOM LITERATURE

God's compassion for the poor is clear throughout the Psalms and other poetic literature in the Old Testament. The marginalized, vulnerable, and oppressed occupy a special place in the heart of God, because they only have Him as their defender and advocate. For example, Psalm 10:17–18, says that "You hear, O Lord, the desire of the afflicted; you encourage them, and you listen to their cry, defending the fatherless and oppressed, in order that man, who is of the earth, may terrify no more." Similarly, in Psalm 82:3–4, God mandates caring for the poor and protecting them from those who would do them harm: "Defend the cause of the weak and fatherless; maintain the rights of the poor and oppressed. Rescue the weak and needy, deliver them from the hand of the wicked."

The Bible's Wisdom Literature (Job through Ecclesiastes) echoes this concern for the poor and oppressed. In fact, care for the poor is considered an indication of how someone values God: "He who oppresses the poor shows contempt for their Maker, but he who is kind to the needy honors God," wrote the wise King Solomon.[20] But another important strand weaves through the wisdom books, that of *individual responsibility for prosperity*. The wisdom books, especially Proverbs, repeatedly make the connection between diligence, hard work, initiative—and prosperity.

For example, Solomon writes, "Lazy hands make a man poor, but diligent hands bring wealth."[21] This is part of a broader point made throughout Proverbs, that a person's individual moral character (or to put it another way, adherence to the way of wisdom) determines the path that person's life takes. The fool, or one who lacks wisdom and character, ends up with a life of calamity, but the wise person, the one who has well-developed character, ends up with a life of prosperity and well-being.

Of course, the Proverbs are rules of thumb and Scripture as a whole acknowledges exceptions to this general pattern—both the poor saint and the rich idiot! And sometimes the poor are poor because they are the victims of injustice.[22] To be sure, this is not teaching anything like a "prosperity theology" in which God always and automatically rewards righteousness with material wealth. Even the Proverbs acknowledge that wealth doesn't last forever (27:24). But the general pattern here is that prosperity is a matter of personal responsibility, namely, hard work, diligence, and perseverance.

Here are some other examples of how frequently the Proverbs make this connection between individual responsibility and prosperity. Wealth from hard work grows over time, and work and initiative brings profit, as opposed to mere talk.[23] Ambition and drive are good things because they motivate a person to work hard to improve his situation. Wise planning and hard work lead to prosperity as opposed to easy shortcuts and get-rich-quick schemes.[24] Foresight, planning, and hard work bring an abundance, as opposed to the person who chases useless fantasies and dreams. By contrast, greed, or ambition that's out of control, ultimately brings a person down to poverty.[25]

The emphasis seems pretty clear—that individual responsibility, a strong work ethic, and other "entrepreneurial" character traits such as initiative and perseverance, are critical to a life of economic prosperity. We'll have a lot more to say about these virtues in chapter 3.

The Proverbs graphically illustrate this point repeatedly with the portrait of the sluggard—the lazy fool who lacks initiative and refuses to take responsibility for his or her own well-being. He is caricatured frequently in Proverbs as being too lazy even to bring his food to his mouth.[26] He makes up outrageous lies to avoid work[27] and is so lazy that he resembles a door turning on its hinges as he turns on his bed, unable to get up and face the day.[28]

Proverbs 24:30–34 depicts the sluggard's field as unproductive, overgrown with weeds and suffering from broken walls, and warns that "a little sleep, a little slumber and folding of the hands to rest—and then poverty will pounce on you like a bandit and scarcity will attack you like an armed robber."

> **Proverbs warns that "a little sleep, a little slumber . . . and then poverty will pounce on you like a bandit."**

The same lesson about laziness and hard work is drawn earlier in the Proverbs, when the diligence and hard work of the ant puts the lazy person to shame, and the conclusion drawn is exactly the same as the telling phrase we quoted just above—"a little sleep, a little slumber . . . and then poverty will pounce on you like an armed bandit. . ." (6:6–11).

As important as these character traits are, it is also important to recognize that a person's prosperity is ultimately a blessing from God. This was particularly true in the agricultural economy of the ancient world. People were dependent on natural forces such as rainfall to have a sufficient harvest. But it is no less true in our information-based economy today. The Proverbs indicate that it's the blessing of God that makes a person prosperous (10:22), and that God is the one who enables us to enjoy the fruit of our labors—and the teacher in Ecclesiastes says that it's a good thing that we can enjoy life as His good gift.[29]

WHAT THE PROPHETS SAY
ABOUT THE POOR AND INJUSTICE

When the prophets come on the scene, the emphasis is back to taking care of the poor. The prophets routinely and forcefully spoke out against oppression, economic injustice, and exploitation of the poor. They considered taking care of the poor a strong indicator of a person's (and the nation Israel's) spiritual health,[30] even making a strong connection between compassion for the poor and genuinely knowing God.[31] The prophets considered this neglect of the poor a serious disregard of the law, and it was one of Israel's primary moral failings.

The prophets spoke passionately against the exploitation of the poor. Ezekiel indicated that the shortcomings of the northern kingdom of Israel included pride, gluttony, and laziness, "while the poor and needy suffered outside her door."[32] Amos indicted the nation for their callous abuse of the vulnerable, pointing out that they sold "honorable people for silver and poor people for a pair of sandals; they trample helpless people in the dust and shove the oppressed out of the way." He made his condemnation even more pointed when he accused "you women who oppress the poor and crush the needy."[33]

The prophet Micah gave a specific illustration of the economic injustices that were commonplace in Israel when he said, "When you want a piece of land you find a way to seize it; when you want someone's house, you take it by fraud and violence; you cheat a man of his property, stealing his family's inheritance."[34] One consequence of their economic exploitation is their own economic ruin, Micah said, using the pointed imagery of God confiscating their land! He indicted them for taking everything from those who had little to begin with: "You steal the shirts right off the backs of those who trusted you; you have evicted women from their homes and forever stripped their children of all that God would give them."[35]

Habakkuk echoed these themes when he accused the people of becoming rich by means of extortion: "you who build big houses with money gained dishonestly" and "you who build cities with money gained through murder and corruption."[36] Instead of taking care of the poor, as the law demanded, they took advantage of them.

ECONOMICS, JESUS, AND THE NEW TESTAMENT

In the New Testament, Jesus took up the same themes as the prophets. The poor were just as important to Jesus as they were to the prophets. When the followers of John the Baptist (who was in prison at the time) asked Jesus if

He was indeed the Messiah who was to come, He answered in terms that could have been taken right out of the prophets. He put it like this, "Go back and report to John what you see and hear—the blind receive sight, the lame walk, those who have leprosy are cured, the deaf hear, the dead are raised, and the good news is preached to the poor."[37]

The evidence that Jesus was who He claimed to be was not only that He did miracles, but who *the beneficiaries of those miracles were—the poor, marginalized, and vulnerable.* Similarly, when He spoke of final judgment and what would separate His true followers from the pretenders, He made it clear that how someone treats the poor is a critical indication of a person's spiritual maturity. This is likely what Jesus meant when He said, "I tell you the truth, whatever you did for one of the least of these brothers [referring to feeding the hungry and taking in the needy], you did for me."[38]

Jesus didn't just talk about how important it was to take care of the poor, He modeled it too. Other than the disciples, Jesus spent the majority of His time with the outcasts of society—lepers, tax collectors, prostitutes, and the poor. He spent little time with those who were highly esteemed by the culture, such as the religious leaders and the rich. He valued the poor for who they were, and told the people that they should esteem them highly too. For example, He said, "When you give a luncheon or dinner, do not invite your friends, your brothers or relatives and or your rich neighbors; if you do, they may invite you back and so you will be repaid. But when you give a banquet, invite the poor, the crippled, the lame, the blind, and you will be blessed. Although they cannot repay yet, you will be repaid at the resurrection of the righteous."[39] Jesus' esteem for the poor and marginalize was part of His broader teaching about the last being first in the kingdom of God.

Consistent with the message of the Wisdom Literature, many of Jesus' parables were drawn from the everyday world of work and economic life. For example, the parable of the sower compared a person's reception of the kingdom of God to scattering seed among different types of soils (and the parable of the wheat and tares is about a field that produces mixed results despite the best efforts of the owner).[40] Other parables compared God's kingdom to fishing, tending sheep, and shrewd business management.[41]

Jesus also compared the kingdom to business, in which resources are effectively put to use in order to generate a profit. This well-known parable of the talents assumes that it's legitimate to seek a profit and to work hard to deploy a person's financial resources to make that happen.[42] It would also seem to assume that accumulating wealth is not intrinsically a problem, though a person should be careful to avoid the predicament of the rich fool, who put his trust in his accumulated wealth.[43]

ECONOMICS AND THE BEGINNING OF THE CHURCH

The early church carried on Jesus' pattern of caring for the poor and marginalized. They cared for the poor mainly through their extraordinary generosity, following Jesus' mandate to share freely with those who had needs.[44] They could not rely on the government to care for their poor since the church was a persecuted minority in the Roman Empire, and since there were not many mechanisms of the state to take care of the poor. And a lot of the early followers of Jesus were quite poor themselves.

We see this extraordinary generosity in action in Acts 2:42–47. The early church is described as "sharing everything they had." They even sold their personal possessions and property in order to meet the needs of the church. This was a purely voluntary sharing of their material goods and not a pattern for any *forced* redistribution of goods, characteristic of socialism. That's not to say that all redistribution of wealth is necessarily wrong, only that Acts 2 does not provide a basis for an economic arrangement like socialism. Part of the reason for this was that in the early church there was no forced renunciation of your property as a condition of membership. But there was unprecedented openhandedness with their goods to meet needs that arose. The main reason for their generosity was that they had been personally transformed by the message of Jesus. Acts 2 provides a model for this kind of personal liberality but has little to say about economic systems themselves.[45]

As in the Old Testament, self-support was assumed in the early church. Self-interest was not condemned, but affirmed, and balanced by concern for the interests of others.[46] The responsibility for providing for your own needs and needs of your family was taken very seriously.

The apostle Paul encouraged a life of diligence in order to provide for self and family, and cautioned those who were not willing to work, when he said, "Those unwilling to work will not get to eat."[47] What he meant by this is that if someone is not willing to work, he or she does not have any claim on the generosity of others.

Paul modeled such a life of self-support, even while he was busy establishing churches, so that he would not be a financial burden on the community. He strongly commands idle people to "settle down and earn the bread they eat." He states this even more strongly when he counsels his understudy Timothy that "anyone who does not provide for his relatives, especially for his immediate family . . . has denied the faith."[48] This kind of personal responsibility for self-support is consistent throughout the Bible, while making room for generosity and provision for those who cannot care for themselves.

THE BIBLE ON POSSESSIONS AND WORK

So let's summarize some of the main elements of the Bible's teaching on economic life, including wealth, poverty, and possessions:

1. The material world is intrinsically good because it's God's good creation, though it is marred by sin.
2. God owns the world's economic resources, and human beings are trustees of those resources, responsible for their careful and productive use.
3. Responsible wealth creation is integrally connected with the dominion mandate and with human beings being made in the image of God.
4. Work/economic activity is fundamentally good, ordained by God.
5. Human beings who are capable of working are responsible for supporting themselves and their dependents.
6. The community is responsible for helping support those who are unable to work.
7. Human beings are not to exploit the economically vulnerable, but to help them support themselves.

THE BIBLE AND ECONOMIC SYSTEMS

Now, after reading all this material from the Bible, you may be wondering what it has to do with economic systems such as capitalism. As we have just seen, the Bible has a lot to say about economic life, even though it is not a textbook on economic systems.

The emphasis in the Bible is on *general principles, not specific policies.*[49] To put it another way, the Bible focuses on the ends of the economic system more than the means for accomplishing those *ends.* There is ongoing debate over the best means to achieve the ends of economics. But the Bible is pretty clear about some of the ends that a just economic system should accomplish.

First, the economic system should *maximize the opportunities for human beings to exercise creativity, initiative, and innovation*—what we might call the "entrepreneurial" traits, or "human capital." These are a key part of what it means for human beings to exercise dominion over creation (to put the resources of the world to responsible and productive use) as those made in God's image. We would suggest that capitalism unleashes human capital better than any other economic system that has ever been tried.

A second clear end of the economic system is *to provide a means for human beings to support themselves and their dependents;* that is, to provide access to the world's productive resources. We would suggest that capitalism provides the best means for the most people to achieve self-support and lift themselves out of poverty. To be sure, there are other conditions necessary for the market system to flourish such as an established system for the rule of law. And there is no doubt that there still remain substantial numbers of people in grinding poverty—roughly three billion of the world's population of 6.8 billion.

But you have to ask, What happened to the *nearly four billion* who are no longer in poverty? They have lifted themselves out of poverty by participation in the economic activity that capitalism generates. Even though globalization has certainly not been all positive, it is largely responsible for lifting millions out of poverty in the developing world.[50] We reject the notion that capitalism causes poverty, a charge that we'll take up in chapter 4.

A third end of the economic system is that *it must take care of those who cannot take care of themselves.* It must provide a safety net for the poor. We would suggest that capitalism is the best system that has been tried for taking care of the poor. Here are two reasons. First, capitalism provides the resources that are necessary for either private charity, or public assistance through taxes, to help support the poor. Both charity and government assistance assume productive wealth creation. Otherwise where do the resources come from to help the poor? But more importantly, capitalism provides the opportunities for the poor to help themselves out of poverty and uphold their dignity at the same time, since they are participants in the system and not simply recipients of charity.

Capitalism provides opportunities for the poor to help themselves out of poverty *and* to uphold their dignity.

Though no one claims that capitalism is without flaws or limits (which we will address in chapters 4 and 8), we suggest that it's the system most consistent with those virtues and principles. It's to a further discussion of those virtues that we turn in the next chapter.

NOTES

1. Quoted in Amanda Carpenter, "Clinton: Something Has to Be Taken Away from Some People," at http://townhall.com/columnists/AmandaCarpenter/2007/06/04/clinton_something_has_to_be_taken_away_from_some_people?page=1. Then-Senator Hillary Clinton was speaking during a nationally televised Faith and Values Forum broadcast on CNN television, June 4, 2007.

2. For further reading on economic life in the ancient world, see D. E. Oakman, "Economics of Palestine," *Dictionary of New Testament Background*, Craig A. Evans and Stanley E. Porter, eds. (Downers Grove, Ill.: InterVarsity, 2000), 303–308. Also see Daniel C. Snell and Steven Sidebotham, "Trade and Commerce," *Anchor Bible Dictionary* (New York: Doubleday, 1997): VI, 625–33.

3. Oakman, "Economics of Palestine," 304.

4. This was one reason why it made so little sense for the rich fool to build bigger barns to store his crops; see Jesus' parable in Luke 12:13–21.

5. See Genesis 1:28–30.

6. See Genesis 2:19–20.

7. See Genesis 1:26–27.

8. Brian Griffiths, *The Creation of Wealth: The Christian's Case for Capitalism* (Downers Grove, Ill.: InterVarsity, 1984), 52–53.

9. As a worker, "God [surveyed] all that he had made" (Genesis 1:31).

10. Genesis 3:17. For further reading on responsible wealth creation, see Kenman L. Wong and Scott B. Rae, *Business as Transformational Service* (Downers Grove, Ill.: InterVarsity, 2010).

11. Exodus 19:5–6.

12. Leviticus 19:35–36; Deuteronomy 25:13–16.

13. Leviticus 25:23.

14. See Deuteronomy 15:1–11; 26:12–13.

15. Leviticus 19:9–10; 25:25–28.

16. See Leviticus 25:8–12. Though the new owner was to restore the land to its original owner during the Jubilee, there is no evidence that such a radical tradition was ever followed.

17. Exodus 16:29; 34:21.

18. For more discussion of this point, see Gordon D. Fee and Douglas Stuart, *How to Read the Bible for All Its Worth* (Grand Rapids: Zondervan, 1981), 65–70, 135–47.

19. There is considerable debate over the meaning of the Jubilee and its application for today. To read more on this, see Christopher J. H. Wright, *Old Testament Ethics for the People of God* (Downers Grove, Ill.: InterVarsity, 2004), 199–210.

20. Proverbs 14:31; see also Proverbs 17:5; 19:17.

21. Proverbs 10:4.

22. Proverbs 13:23.

23. Proverbs 14:23.

24. Proverbs 13:11; 16:26; 20:13; 28:20.

25. Proverbs 28:19, 22, 25.

26. Proverbs 19:24; 26:15.

27. "There is a lion in streets!" is his outlandish alibi (Proverbs 22:13; 26:13).

28. Proverbs 26:14.

29. Ecclesiastes 2:24–25; 5:18–20.

30. Isaiah 58:6–7.

31. Jeremiah 22:16.

32. Ezekiel 16:49 NLT.

33. Amos 2:6–7 NLT and 4:1, respectively.

34. Micah 2:2 NLT.

35. Micah 3:4, 8–9 NLT.

36. Habakkuk 2:6, 9, 12 NLT.

37. Matthew 11:4–5.

38. Matthew 25:40.

39. Luke 14:12–14.

40. Matthew 13:1–23.

41. Matthew 13:47–52; Luke 15:1–7; 16:1–9.

42. Matthew 25:14–30; Luke 19:11–26.

43. See Luke 12:13–21.

44. Luke 10:25–37; 12:33.

45. To read more on the sharing of resources in the early church, see Justo L. Gonzalez, *Faith and Wealth* (New York: HarperCollins, 1990), 79–86.

46. Philippians 2:4.

47. 2 Thessalonians 3:10 NLT; see 1 Thessalonians 4:11–12.

48. 2 Thessalonians 3:12 and 1 Timothy 5:8, respectively.

49. Griffiths, *The Creation of Wealth*, 48.

50. For statistics just since 1970, see Indur M. Goklany, *The Improving State of the World* (Washington, D.C.: Cato Institute, 2007). These suggest that close to 1.6 billion people emerged from poverty during this time, and the correlation between economic freedom and rising out of poverty is unmistakable.

Virtue: moral excellence; goodness

—AMERICAN CENTURY DICTIONARY, FOURTH EDITION

ANCIENT VIRTUES
in the
MODERN MARKETPLACE

False accounting practices. Securities fraud. "Predatory" mortgage lenders. Car companies mismanaged into bankruptcy. Deceptive credit card agreements. A quick review of news reports on any given day during the recession of 2008–2009 could have easily led one to believe that business people are all greedy, and that America's system of *capitalism* is the most corrupt economic system on the planet.

But to evaluate capitalism based exclusively on day-to-day press coverage is a huge mistake. Media reports, generally speaking, only provide a snapshot in time, and those "snapshots" are often, by intention, critical and controversial. After all, controversy and conflict sell.

The fact is that, on a day-to-day basis, most business transactions are executed correctly, most participants in our economy work hard and play by the rules, and things generally go well. (If this were not true, our economy would not be as functional as it is.)

The very fact that activity in our capitalistic economy usually happens the way it's supposed to illustrates something very important. It suggests that, somehow, participants in our free-market economy are informed and influenced by a common reservoir of values. True, our American society is diverse and complex; and nearly every ethnicity, religious tradition, and socioeconomic class can be found somewhere within the United States. Yet, somehow, most participants in the American economy, whether immigrants from another part of the world or citizens who have lived here all their lives, find their way in our capitalistic economy, and find an incentive to behave well and to do right by others in their day-to-day affairs.

The relative cohesiveness within our economy is significant, in and of itself. But media coverage of the economy and day-to-day activities aside, capitalism can be evaluated accurately only when viewed in its proper context. This involves examining capitalism next to other economic systems, and with a view toward world history. Only in this way can one begin to accurately see the benefits of capitalism in the United States and around the world during the past couple of centuries.

What about the scandalous problems listed at the start of this chapter? Yes, they are serious. They raise a lot of questions, and the questions demand responses. And we will offer our responses to these and other questions later in the book. For now, we want to focus on a core set of moral virtues that are both required within a society for a capitalistic economic system to exist in the first place, and are then to continue and ultimately flourish within a society.

Recognizing the existence of these virtues within a capitalistic economic system may well be the most important and persuasive element in a general defense of capitalism.

We understand why the skeptics are wary of capitalism; they have observed bad behavior or unfortunate circumstances from afar or firsthand. Some readily accept that capitalism has lifted more people out of poverty. They know it has produced more wealth for more people around the world than any other economic system ever known. Yet they argue, "Capitalism is unfair" or "Capitalism is immoral." Many Americans reading about the 2008–2009 recession are thinking and saying these kinds of things. While the American lifestyle remains, on a whole, materially superior to the lifestyles experienced in many other countries, economic injustices still exist, and capitalism is often blamed for those injustices.

WHY VIRTUE IS IMPORTANT

Such questioning of the virtues found in capitalism is a good thing for at least a couple of reasons. For one, it illustrates that our society still embodies a collective moral conscience. It may be easy, even common, for some Americans to lament what they perceive to be the "moral decay" in our society, or the decline of our social fabric. But if the United States were truly as amoral or immoral as some would have us believe, we wouldn't be having discussions and debates about people's perceptions of injustice.

Second, moral questions about the economy also remind us of an important part of the nature and essence of the human person. As humans we are, of course, material beings, and we quite naturally need and want material sustenance and reward. And along with this, we are relational beings, in that we need and want to share our lives in relationships that are beneficial to us.

But we are also moral beings. From the Judeo-Christian viewpoint, humans have been *made in the image of God.* And while none of us is perfect, and nobody does the right thing all the time, being "made in the image of God" implies, in part, that we are creatures who gener-ally desire justice and goodness. According to the Scrip-ture, we all have "the law written on our hearts."[1] That is, we have a basic and built-in understanding of right and wrong. And it is this very desire that motivates our moral questioning.

Capitalism seeks to bring out the best from each individual.

So what does capitalism have to do with justice and fairness and other virtues? Quite a bit. As we make our way through these simple, ancient virtues, some will be tempted to protest and say that we are being terribly idealistic in our assumptions. But this is, at least in part, the point we are making. Capitalism unapologetically begins with some very high ideals in mind, and seeks to bring out the best from each individual.

When we say that "capitalism brings out the best" in people, we mean that in a couple of different ways. For one, capitalism gives people an incentive to pursue excellence. But beyond that, capitalism creates an environment that, as philosopher Adam Smith envisioned, allows self-interest to be harnessed in such a way that it promotes the "common good."[2] We'll address these and capitalism's other high ideals as we progress through this chapter, and later in the book we'll confront the reality that sometimes the ideals are not achieved. But for now, let's consider some of the many "moral goods" that are embodied within, and sustained by, the economic system of capitalism.

SOCIETAL STABILITY

Though technically not a virtue, one of the most important features of capitalism is societal stability, a moral good that directly impacts the life of the individual person, as well as society collectively. Of course, many of the virtues found in capitalism impact people both individually and collectively. But for our purposes here, we'll start with something that is desirable for entire societies, the moral good of stability.

When prices of goods rise and currency values fall, when the stock market plummets and personal retirement accounts shrink, when businesses declare bankruptcy and unemployment increases—in times such as these, it's difficult for some to connect the word *capitalism* with the idea of stability. But during the past two hundred years or so, the capitalist, free-market economic system has been at the center of some of the most stable and cohesive societies ever known to mankind.

One of the reasons for this is that capitalism remains the preferred economic system, even the necessary economic system, for any society that upholds a true sense of human rights. History has shown us that the societies that do best with human rights are led by a government that is ultimately controlled by the very people who, themselves, are the governed. And no system of government allows for more participation by the governed than an elective democracy.

By definition, *a democracy* is a system of government wherein the power to govern ultimately rests with private citizens. The governed, which includes every citizen in the society, exercise their "power" collectively by choosing the individuals who will be their governors, usually by means of free elections. And while American-styled democracy has been a model for other nations, democracy has nonetheless emerged in a variety of other forms around the world. We won't get into all the various nuances of democracy here. But one point we'll make: After roughly five thousand years of civilization and centuries of experiments wherein societies have been ruled by an individual, or by a small group of individuals, or by a particular "social class" or religious group, history has taught us that the societies which grant ultimate authority to its citizens are the societies that treat people the best, and are the most stable.

HOW CAPITALISM TRANSFORMED EUROPE

But what does a preference for elective democracy have to do with capitalism and societal stability? To better understand the connection, it's helpful to take a brief look at precapitalist Europe, and the ways in which capitalism has transformed and stabilized that region of the world.

While democracy is essential for a society to attain both stability and humane treatment of its citizens, it is not in and of itself sufficient. People will not remain content to simply cast a vote and elect new leaders every few years if they're stuck living in destitute conditions with no hope of improvement. Indeed, human beings have a natural longing to be free—free to risk and to try new things, free to make their own decisions, free to better themselves, free to improve their circumstances. In terms of material sustenance and prosperity, a society needs individuals to be free to risk, to create, and to innovate, to ensure that its economy remains vibrant and provides adequate opportunity. Precapitalist England illustrates what happens in a society when this kind of "economic freedom" is missing.

For several centuries during the medieval period of history, England existed largely as a "feudalist" society. Although England still had a king, a queen, and its national legislative body known as the Parliament (which eventually would emerge as a freely elected, law-making body), the ultimate control of the country, economically and otherwise, rested in the hands of "lords." The lords were wealthy citizens who controlled their own territorial regions, managed their own estates, administered their own justice, levied their own taxes, and demanded allegiance, and even military service, from their underlings. It was a society of rich and poor. The lords lived aristocratic lifestyles among their family and friends, while the poor, known at the time as "serfs," weren't well connected and made their way in life working for the lords. This type of societal structure didn't allow for what we would think of today as a middle class, and those who lived under feudalism certainly knew their place in the world.

The structure of feudalism remained in place in England for several centuries, until it eventually ran into trouble. The individual lords, who essentially controlled all of the land and agricultural resources within their territories, did not compete with agricultural suppliers outside their territories. Without the challenge of competition, they had no incentive to invest time and energy in new, innovative ways of improving agricultural production. Without technological innovation, production eventually reached a plateau. As agricultural production began to stagnate under the control of the lords, England also encountered periods of bad weather, which created famines and plagues and brought about massive death and labor shortages. With all these crises, the control over the nation's people and wealth that the lords—the aristocratic, wealthy class in England—had maintained for so long became unstable. Agricultural production needed to expand, yet the labor pool was shrinking. The lords soon reached a point where their control over their nation's resources and people was threatened.

With all these crises, the control by the wealthy class became unstable.

In an increasingly unstable society, as the lords sought to grow their fortunes by stealing from one another and conquering one another, wars became common. Great scholars and philosophers of the era (such as Machiavelli) wrote eloquently about the "art" of war and power, and believed that prosperity was achieved by controlling as much land and as many material goods as possible. And while all this transpired, the serfs became pawns in the militaristic gamesmanship of the lords. Thus England, as well as much of Europe, became very unstable.[3]

Against this backdrop of predatory, warmongering tendencies from the lords and the European nations, philosophers like David Hume and Adam Smith began challenging people to think differently.[4] Prosperity, these thinkers surmised, was not found in warfare and the raw pursuit of power. (Indeed, Smith in particular believed that war impoverishes a nation.) On the contrary, these philosophers believed that the key to a virtuous, prosperous, stable society was to focus not on war and conquest, but rather, to focus on creating abundance. And to create a necessary level of abundance, they reasoned, people must be free to pursue their own, personal self-interest, and must be free to engage their creativity, in order that the society would benefit from their invention and innovation.

A NEW WAY OF THINKING

Some of the early impact of this "new way of thinking" resulted in the serfs being permitted to sell their labor and talents for the best price they could get, to the lords and landowners for whom they worked. This gave the lower class the opportunity to improve their circumstances, which in turn provided an incentive for them to work harder and find better, more efficient, more innovative ways of doing things. And as Smith continued to write and publish, he expanded on these early ideas, arguing that not only should individuals be free to sell their products and services, but that they should also be free to compete with each other. This type of competition, he believed, created an incentive to keep prices of goods and services as low as possible (which was a benefit to the consumer), but also created an incentive for product and service providers to find better, more creative, more effective ways of doing things.[5]

It would be many decades after the 1776 publication of Adam Smith's renowned work *The Wealth of Nations* before this new, competitive, free-market economic system would be labeled "capitalism." But the early ideas of Smith and several of his contemporaries helped bring about the transition from the medieval emphasis of war and conquest to a new era focused on liberation and creating abundance. These ideas and principles led to a more stable and prosperous Europe, but they also helped lay the groundwork for the early beginnings of the United States of America.

Those alive today need only look back on the events of the past sixty years to see how the personal economic freedom of capitalism has transformed entire regions of the world. The level of freedom afforded by individual governments to private citizens and business owners varies from one country to another. But the peaceable revolution brought about by capitalism has been at the epicenter of the historically unprecedented creation of wealth in the United States, as well as the relative prosperity and stability in the nations of Japan, South Korea, Singapore, Israel, and India, to name a few. Conversely, today's most unstable, vicious, and dangerous nations offer very little, if any, economic freedom to their citizens, and seek to do damage to other nations as a means of conquest and survival.

When humans are free to create and innovate, they can focus on achieving the abundance they need, rather than on taking from others. This is what *New York Times* columnist Thomas Friedman calls "the golden arches theory of conflict prevention." He correctly describes how costly conflict is in terms of business, globally integrated supply chains, and customer relationships. It's for this reason that global capitalism (including McDonald's golden arches in more than 120 countries) has contributed to social stability.[6] This is good for individuals, and it is good for entire societies. Thus, one of the great achievements entailed in capitalism is the good of societal stability. And when this good is present in a society, it enables a variety of virtues to flourish.

VIRTUE 1: CREATIVITY

At the center of the capitalist economic system is the elevation of human creativity. As we saw in the example of precapitalist England, a society suffers with both a material poverty and a poverty of the human spirit when it either ignores or stifles the capacity for individual humans to create and innovate. And capitalism not only affirms and encourages human creativity, it relies upon it as well. A society needs at least some of its members to continually be discovering better ways of accomplishing the established tasks, while at the same time developing new tasks, so as to create products and services and means of doing things that have yet to exist. Without such individuals, an economic system stagnates, and the broader society suffers.

Does your life's work encourage and reward creativity? If we are honest, some of us would have to answer "no" to that question. Repetitive, routine tasks, combined with a workplace that doesn't seem to offer the possibility of advancement, can quickly become mundane and lead to some serious "job dissatisfaction." If your work history is characterized by these kinds of frustrations, it may be difficult to believe that our system of capitalism places much of an emphasis on creativity at all.

But a more careful examination—both of the economy as a whole and one's individual situation—will likely tell a different story. No matter how undesirable a particular "job" or task may be in the modern American economy, chances are that the particular task in question didn't even exist in previous generations. Likewise, if the job did exist in the past, more than likely the performance of that job has become more efficient, more safe, and less burdensome over time. How can this be the case? It is because of the presence of human creativity.

No matter what a particular work setting may involve, be it heavy machinery, sophisticated electronic technology, or the land and the earth's elements, it nonetheless entails physical matter. But without human creativity, the machinery, the technology, and the land amount to nothing more than mere physical matter.

It's interesting to note that the word *capital* itself comes from the Latin word *caput*, which means *head*. This refers to the human and intellectual elements of creating capital out of the earth's resources (for example, using sand to make silicon). Thus, it is human creativity that creates the devices, works the land, and produces something of value with them. The involvement of the human person makes all the difference.

And what, exactly, is "human creativity," as we are considering it here? In one sense, it is simply as we have described it—to make something of value. But from a Judeo-Christian vantage point, the capacity to create is something distinctly human, something God-given, and something indicative of the unique nature of the human person, having been "made in the image of God." While some animals have the capacity to create things (for example, birds build nests), they nonetheless do so in a repetitive fashion, and based upon their innate instincts. Human individuals, on the other hand, have the unique capacity to meet their needs, and the needs of others, in continually new and innovative ways. Capitalism requires this kind of action, rewards it when it occurs, and in so doing, encourages it to continue.

VIRTUE 2: INITIATIVE

For some people, the idea of personal initiative may be regarded as more of a vice than a virtue. Critics may suggest that having initiative can lead to "being overly independent" or having an "independent mind-set," and this can interfere with a society's need to create a sense of cohesiveness or community. Still others claim that initiative necessarily leads to selfish and excessive consumption, which in turn threatens to deplete the world's supply of energy, food, and other essential resources. Initiative, from this perspective, places the personal preferences of the individual above all other considerations in a society, and therefore leads to a calloused, cruel world where the "collective good" is neglected.

While some of these social ills are legitimate and real, they are not necessarily caused by people exercising "too much initiative." Additionally, it is inaccurate to assume that for one to have initiative necessarily means that one is being excessive in their initiative, or being greedy, or that one is being independent at the expense of others. To better understand initiative as a virtue, it's necessary to contrast it with dependence.

Recall that in our examination of precapitalist Europe, the poor citizens in that society, the serfs, were completely dependent on the rich, ruling lords. While the lords controlled essentially all the economic resources that existed, the serfs had no hope of becoming owners themselves, and thus would never be able to break out of their cycle of dependency. It wasn't until the implementation of the "free market reforms" envisioned by Adam Smith and David Hume, granting serfs the ability to charge money for their labor, that serfs had a chance to transcend their lives of servile dependency and create independent lives of their own.

Capitalism requires people to function independently of others, and this is a good thing. While it is true that every role within the economy is different, and therefore the demands placed upon individuals are different, nonetheless this demand for independence generally requires a person, to some degree or another, to take risks and make decisions, to invest and develop their God-given talents, to master certain essential life skills, and to engage those talents and skills for their own benefit and for the benefit of others.

In short, the demand for initiative in our economy helps to enable human development and maturity, rather than allowing people (or requiring them) to live well into their adult years with a childlike reliance on others. Independent adults, in turn, are better able to create material abundance and economic opportunity for themselves and others, raise children more effectively, and be charitable with the poor and needy. The virtue of independence is balanced with the virtues of service and cooperation, and this balance creates the necessary interdependence for broad prosperity.

VIRTUE 3: COOPERATION

Cooperation and *initiative* may seem like competing forces within a society, as though one works against the other. But societies require both, and just as capitalism requires and reinforces initiative, it does the same with the virtue of cooperation.

In our review of the feudal society of Europe prior to capitalism, we saw a clearly marked dividing line between rich and poor. In feudal England, while some basic human rights regarding the treatment of the serfs were largely upheld, the two social classes were significantly isolated from each other. The wealthy primarily chose to order their personal lives among themselves, enjoying their lives of wealth, high culture, and refinement; the serfs had little opportunity to involve themselves in such environments. The interaction that did take place between the serfs and the wealthy placed the serfs in a disadvantaged, dependent position.

Capitalism changes this. Rather than defining and limiting people according to the socioeconomic "class" into which they were born, capitalism extends opportunity to every individual, and enables upward mobility. But not only does capitalism extend opportunity to all, it has also brought about an unprecedented transformation of the world's social fabric, because of its tendency to break down social barriers and unite people for the common cause of commerce. Today, to a greater degree than at any other time in history, social classes around the world intermingle in the open marketplace of free enterprise.

Such cooperation is so commonplace in the United States today that we tend to overlook it or ignore it. But consider for a moment: Are some people in your workplace richer than others? Do your associates come from diverse personal backgrounds and upbringings? What about the people who work in the stores and businesses where you purchase goods and services? Most of us, especially those of us who live in a big city or suburban setting, are interacting with people from diverse cultural and socioeconomic backgrounds every day. We may have little in common with our colleagues and associates, apart from the time we spend together in our workplace or interacting at a store or restaurant, and the time we do spend engaged in such business transactions may be the only time in our lives that we cross paths with people of different backgrounds, social classes, and so forth. Nonetheless, capitalistic free-market enterprise requires cooperation. It brings people together—rich, poor, middle class, the well educated, the poorly educated, and all the rest—for the purposes of accomplishing common objectives. The remarkable thing about capitalism is the degree of cooperation required by otherwise self-interested individuals, and how we take this for granted on a daily basis.

VIRTUE 4: CIVILITY

When Adam Smith imagined how to restructure a society's economy, he envisioned that interjecting competition into the marketplace would force all the participants in the market to become better people. Business owners, faced with the prospect of their workers and customers leaving to accept a "better offer" elsewhere, would have to treat them both with a greater level of dignity and respect. Workers, faced with a competitive labor supply, would have to develop better skills at dealing with customers, and would also have to do their part at building better relationships with the people for whom they worked. In short, a competitive marketplace would demand a greater level of civility from all its participants, and those who refused to become more civil and refined in their approach to work would lose economic opportunity.

The level of civility in an economy may vary. You may have horror stories to tell about a terrible environment you once worked in, or perhaps you've had an unpleasant experience as a customer of a particular business or industry. But while civility in the marketplace varies, it does exist; and when people in a capitalistic system don't behave in a civil fashion, it can harm their financial prospects.

The average workplace in any field requires some level of etiquette, an ability to understand other people and their needs, a willingness to serve other people, the ability to be patient with other people, and a willingness to overlook other people's flaws and mistakes. Thus most of us who participate in the free-market economy have to develop some level of these traits and inculcate them into our daily work. If we don't, we suffer the consequences of diminished opportunity. Likewise, most of us notice quite quickly when we are functioning in the role of a customer or client, and a product or service provider does not emulate these traits for us.

Clearly, then, prosperity demands the virtue of civility. Sellers certainly don't have to "love their neighbors" or even like them, but to succeed, businesses must serve them well and treat them with respect. Companies that fail to treat their customers well will soon find themselves out of business. Capitalism demands the virtues of civility and nurtures it at the same time.

However problematic or unpleasant any given workplace or transaction might be, capitalism has nonetheless moved us far away from the indifference, aggression, and even outright cheating of the precapitalist era, to a point where we are beholden to emulate civility, and we also expect to be treated well. The competition of capitalism has thus helped to cultivate civility.

VIRTUE 5: RESPONSIBILITY

When it comes to parenting, most would agree that it's best to raise kids in such a way that they grow up to demonstrate personal responsibility. When it comes to growing and nurturing a society, we all benefit when people live lives of personal responsibility. There are plenty of experts who can tell you how to encourage personal responsibility with your kids. But how does a society, collectively speaking, encourage personal responsibility among its members?

Capitalism is one way. From the start, the "rules" of capitalism say, in part, that if you do a day's work, you earn a day's pay. Conversely, if you don't perform your job satisfactorily on a day-to-day basis, you probably won't continue to get paid for very long. This market reality creates a tremendous incentive for responsible behavior.

Some argue that capitalism's excessive focus on individual responsibility can lead to a cruel society. This is a legitimate concern, and we certainly don't argue for a society that is devoid of any social safety net. But in terms of advancing virtue, capitalism generally demands that we do well by producing goods and services that meet the needs of others, rewards us when we do well, and becomes our incentive to continue to do well. This cycle produces tremendous good for the individual person, as well as the broad society.

Recall that in our examination of precapitalist Europe, we learned that economic productivity in the society eventually reached a plateau. This was, in part, because nobody had incentives to increase the quantities of production, but also because nobody was held responsible to make that happen. It was understood in that society that serfs would work and serve the lords, but the lords were also expected to take care of the serfs and provide for them. The rule of "a day's pay for a day's work" wasn't in place in precapitalist Europe, the way it is in our modern, capitalist economic system. And the presence of that rule helps to create both a responsible society and a productive society. Even in more recent history, the lack of productivity has been apparent within economic systems that have not held people responsible for their behavior and performance.

Capitalism, by design, allows us to succeed *and* to fail.

The former Soviet Union met its demise for a variety of reasons, but at the heart of it all was the inability of its economic system to produce adequately. And why couldn't the economy produce? Because the government controlled nearly everything for its people—what kind of work a person did, where they would live, where and when they would acquire goods for their household, and so forth. With government controlling so much of people's lives, individual persons had little responsibility for their lives. And when people are not left to be responsible for their lives, they become unproductive and are thus left with little incentive to improve their lives.

One of the obvious implications in this facet of capitalism is the reality that if you don't do a day's work, you probably won't get a day's pay. That is, while capitalism creates an incentive for us to do well and rewards us when we do, it also allows us to experience the consequences of our choices when we choose not to do well. In short, capitalism, by design, allows us to succeed *and* to fail. By allowing the individual person to experience the full range of outcomes produced by their choices, capitalism advances the virtue of responsibility for the entire society.

These are some of the main virtues and moral goods that are required, and sustained, by capitalism. Though they are not new, the relatively new development of the capitalistic economic system has nurtured them and made them more commonplace than ever before.

But the sustaining of these goods and virtues is not guaranteed. They can be undermined, both by bad public policy (as we'll examine in chapter 6), and by bad behavior among participants in the economy (as we'll see in chapter 7). Thus, while we can celebrate the moral goodness that capitalism has to offer, we must also recognize that this goodness must be safeguarded by the prudent behavior of individuals, and the guidance of wise public policy.

NOTES

1. See Romans 2:14–16.

2. Adam Smith, *An Inquiry into the Nature and Causes of the Wealth of Nations*, book II (Indianapolis: Liberty Press, 1981).

3. John Cannon, *The Oxford Companion to British History* (New York: Oxford Univ. Press, 2003), 852.

4. Michael Novak, "Wealth and Virtue: The Moral Case for Capitalism," *National Review Online*, 18 February 2004, http:www.nationalreview.com/novak/200402180913.asp.

5. Adam Smith, *The Theory of Moral Sentiments* (1759; repr., New York: Oxford Univ. Press, 1984), part II.

6. For further reading in this area, see Thomas L. Friedman, *The Lexus and the Olive Tree* (New York: Anchor, 1999), 248–75. Friedman also recognizes that nations go to war for a variety of reasons, economic interest being only one of them. Thus "globalization does not end geopolitics."

Socialism . . . that's the way to save the planet, capitalism is the road to hell. . . . Let's fight against capitalism and make it obey us.

—Hugo Chavez, president of Venezuela, speaking at a United Nations' conference

CAPITALISM
and
ITS CRITICS

D o the remarks on the opposite page seem extreme? Hugo Chavez is the freely elected president of Venezuela, yet he frequently expresses his opposition to capitalism.[1] And his antagonism toward free-market economics became a central point of a speech he delivered at the United Nations' Conference on Global Warming in December 2009.

He spoke those words at the UN conference just as we were completing this book. Chavez is not alone in his disdain for capitalism. His perspective is increasingly echoed by people throughout the world, including people here in the United States. "Capitalism is evil," said Michael Moore in his 2009 movie, *Capitalism: A Love Story*. Writer and filmmaker Moore, who also produced *Bowling for Columbine* and *Fahrenheit 9/11*, offered his critique of capitalism just two months before Chavez's attack.

Capitalism: A Love Story is not Moore's first film with an economic theme. In 1989, he released *Roger and Me*, the sad story of what happened to his hometown of Flint, Michigan, when a General Motors plant closed. And he followed this with his book *Downsize This!*, which criticized companies for layoffs and restructuring.

In *Capitalism*, Moore draws a stark conclusion—that capitalism is evil, that it's responsible for the meltdown in the financial markets of 2008–2009, and that it needs to be replaced. When GM finally declared bankruptcy, Moore blamed the automaker for being "a corporation that ruined my hometown and brought misery, divorce, alcoholism, homelessness, physical and mental debilitation, and drug addiction to the people I grew up with."[2]

What an indictment of the company! To be sure, General Motors deserves its share of blame for decades of mismanagement—but for Moore, the blame goes beyond GM to what he believes are the evils of capitalism.

As we have argued, we believe that capitalism is the economic system that fits best with both the Bible and some important and widely shared virtues. Remember, we are comparing capitalism not with the ideal of perfection, but with other comparable economic systems.

THE CRITICS HAVE THEIR SAY

Capitalism does have its share of critics, and they have come out with a vengeance during the economic recession of the late 2000s. Such criticism is not new; in fact, capitalism has a long history of distinguished critics. Well before the Industrial Revolution, medieval philosophers and theologians were skeptical of business and commerce, and before them, some early Christian church leaders viewed all commerce as evil. The Reformers legitimized business as a "worldly calling" from God, in which people could honor their Creator and succeed financially at the same time. But the abuses and excesses of early industrial capitalism reignited the critics. From Charles Dickens in England to the preachers of the so-called social gospel in the United States, the capitalistic economic system was under fire.

After the fall of the Berlin Wall and the collapse of Soviet communism in 1989, many people assumed that the debate over economic systems was essentially over and that capitalism had carried the day. But if advocates of capitalism expected an end of the criticism of the market system, they had another think coming. It seemed that, since capitalism was the only economic system left standing (except for places like Cuba and North Korea), the moral scrutiny directed at the system intensified. It was as though critics and proponents alike were insisting that if capitalism was now the default economic system, we had better get it right and avoid the excesses of the past.

That was the prevailing perspective twenty years ago. Today criticisms of capitalism are again on the front pages of newspapers, inside major news magazines, and on Internet blogs. Many blame the deregulation of financial markets for the 2008–2009 recession and the near collapse of the global financial system.

British executive Sir Martin Sorrell stated bluntly, "Capitalism messed up, or to be more precise, capitalists did."[3] Economics commentator Martin Wolf put it this way: "Another ideological god has failed (referring to free market capitalism). . . . The legitimacy of the market will weaken."[4] Some are suggesting that the state-run capitalism of nations like China is the model of the future, not the United States' free-market version.[5]

Let's consider some of the most common criticisms of capitalism. Many of these condemnations of capitalism have a long history, though some have been reframed after the recent near collapse of the financial markets.

The five common indictments of capitalism are: (1) capitalism is based on greed; (2) the rich get richer at the expense of the poor; (3) capitalism leads to overconsumption and materialism; (4) capitalism leads to gross inequalities in wealth; and (5) the boom and bust cycles endemic to capitalism have painful human costs.

"IT'S ALL ABOUT GREED"

The first and most common criticism of capitalism is that it is a system "based on greed." In his most recent film, Michael Moore goes so far as to accuse capitalism of being a system of "legalized greed." Most people regard greed as a vice (it's one of the seven deadly sins!) and the Bible clearly condemns greed—it regularly appears in the lists of vices in the Bible.[6] Jesus warned His followers to "beware of every form of greed."[7] Thus, the argument about capitalism goes something like this: If greed is a vice, which it is, and capitalism is based on greed, then capitalism must be immoral. Certain religious leaders make this charge frequently, insisting that capitalism is based on the "greed principle"[8] and that capitalist culture glorifies greed.[9] The goal of capitalism often is described as profit maximization, which, critics say, is just another way of describing corporate greed.

One way to respond to this charge is to insist that greed is not a vice—in fact, this is the response of both Gordon Gekko (the fictitious character from the 1987 movie *Wall Street*) and philosopher Ayn Rand. Gekko, whose character is loosely based on the former Wall Street tycoon Ivan Boesky, said that "greed, for lack of a better word, is good—greed is right, greed works." His lines in the movie script came out of a speech that Boesky gave in the mid-1980s at the University of California at Berkeley Business School, in which he insisted that greed is good. Many people believe that this view came directly from Adam Smith's *The Wealth of Nations*, the classic on politics and economics first published in 1776—that Smith himself believed and taught that greed was good.[10]

Rand, on the other hand, developed a version of what is commonly known as ethical egoism—a philosophical system that glorifies the pursuit of self-interest and equates altruism and pity with weakness.[11] Rand was an unabashed enthusiast for capitalism, having grown up in communist Russia, and was not shy about saying that the basis of capitalism was greed, and that this was commendable.[12] Most people, understandably, have a lot of difficulty with the notion that greed is good, since it's not hard to make the case that greed is corrosive to an individual's soul (see Ebenezer Scrooge) and destructive to others.

A second way to respond to the charge that capitalism is based on greed is to insist that greed is *not* the basis for capitalism—something else is, perhaps self-interest, but that's not the same thing as greed. This is more the view of Adam Smith, who was not an economist but a moral philosopher attempting to apply his view of morality to economic life. Yet even for Smith, there was more to it than simply self-interest—that was one of several motivations that were necessary for the market system to function properly.

> **Greed is fundamentally a matter of the human heart, not of any economic system.**

The charge of greed is misplaced because it aims at the wrong target. Greed is fundamentally a matter of the human heart, not of any economic system. Greed can and does flourish in any economic arrangement because greed is a constant human temptation. Of course, greed comes out in capitalism. But greed is hardly unique to capitalism. In fact, greed flourished under various forms of socialism, and avarice is often the most blatant among dictatorships in the developing world.

While the critics of capitalism may eventually agree that greed is indeed a matter of the heart, they would likely insist that greed is much more of a problem in capitalist systems than in any others. But notice that this is different from the claim that capitalism is *based* on greed. The temptations to greed may be more acute in systems that generate wealth as capitalism does because the possibilities for accumulating wealth are greater. But when wealth is being created and people have more resources, the possibilities for charity are also greater, because people have more resources at their disposal.

The United States, which has a very free economy compared to much of the world, is easily the most charitable nation on earth. Its citizens give at a rate of more than double the next closest nation.[13] In addition, when wealth is being created and people can genuinely better their financial situations (which is much more possible in free-market economies), the temptations for greed, envy, and covetousness may actually be diminished. That's because people have confidence that if they work hard, they will be better off in the future than they are today.

The vices of greed, envy, and covetousness can also flourish in systems that make upward mobility difficult—people envy their neighbors when they feel stuck and can't get ahead. The Bible was written within a culture where upward mobility was virtually nonexistent, so the Bible commends contentment and has little to say regarding ambition. The opposite of contentment in the Bible is not ambition, but envy/covetousness.[14]

Let's look more closely at the charge that greed is the basis for capitalism. It's often assumed that greed is the same thing as self-interest. But greed is not the same as self-interest. Self-interest is nothing more than looking out for your own interests, and surely the desire to better yourself is not necessarily being greedy. Of course, the desire to better one's self to the level of someone like Bill Gates—that may be greedy.

> **A desire to better yourself is not necessarily being greedy.**

The Bible is very helpful in making this distinction. The New Testament does not condemn self-interest. It actually commends a person's self-interest but mandates that it be balanced by a concern for the interests of others. For example, the apostle Paul wrote, "Look not only to your own interests, but also to the interests of others."[15] As we mentioned in chapter 2, the Bible directs people to pay sufficient attention to their self-interest so that their needs and the needs of their families are met. There is nothing intrinsically wrong with someone pursuing their self-interest, as long as it is balanced and within limits.

Again, Adam Smith did not believe self-interest is the same thing as greed or that "greed is good." He distinguished between self-interest, which was legitimate, and selfishness, which he viewed as evil.

In *The Wealth of Nations* Smith wrote, "It is not from the benevolence of the butcher, the brewer, or the baker, that we expect our dinner, but from their regard for their own interest. We address ourselves, not to their humanity, but to their self-love, and never talk to them of our own necessities, but of their advantages."[16] Some conclude from this classic statement that it's the greed of the producer that brings society its goods/services, and that the pursuit of individual greed will result in the advance of the common good. They infer that Smith believed that greed was good.

However, this segment from Smith needs to be read with his developed moral philosophy clearly in mind. Remember, Smith was not an economist, but a moral philosopher by training. In his work *The Theory of Moral Sentiments* (written before *The Wealth of Nations*), he argued that human beings were motivated by what he called the "social passions," and that justice, prudence, and benevolence were also key components to governing a person's pursuit of self-interest.

He also defended the ideas of cooperation and sympathy as part of the social passions, which he considered equally as influential on a person as self-interest. The butcher, brewer, and baker all needed cooperation in addition to self-interest in order to flourish. Baron de Montesquieu, one of Smith's contemporaries and fellow advocate of the free market, captured this well. He said something that sounds remarkable today, that "commerce polishes and softens barbaric ways, as we can see every day."[17]

But remember, for much of the history of civilization, human beings often resorted to violence in order to obtain the goods and services they needed. Smith saw an economic system based on trade and mutual advantage as a great improvement over the way goods and services had been distributed in most of the history of civilization.

Finally, Smith advocated an "enlightened self-interest" in which a person possessed the internal resources necessary to provide checks and balances on his or her self-interest. It's not just because these traits are necessary for maximizing long-term self-interest that Smith advocated them—it's also because for Smith they are a part of human nature as a rational person.[18]

"THE RICH GET RICHER AT THE EXPENSE OF THE POOR"

A second very common criticism of capitalism is that the prosperity of the wealthy actually causes the poverty of the poor. This is what people usually mean when they lament that "the rich get richer and the poor get poorer." That is, the prosperity of the wealthy *brings about* the poverty of the poor. You can see this allegation especially in regard to the global economy—that the wealth of the rich nations has come at the expense of the poor nations (although it's also a common theme here in the United States as it pertains to "rich" and "poor" individuals and communities).

Some even accuse the developed world of theft from the developing world. For example, the Episcopal activist Richard Gillett asks rhetorically, "Is this [globalization] expansion dependent upon the existence of a large marginalized sector of the world for its profitability? Is this expansion in some way *causative* of increased impoverishment?"[19] Meanwhile, Catholic Bishop Thomas Gumbleton declares, "The problem with the international global economy is that the wealth of the world goes from the poor to the rich. The rich get richer and the poor get poorer."[20]

While we admit that the persistence of global poverty and the inequality between rich and poor are serious issues, particularly in the poorest parts of the world (where we would argue that free-market principles have yet to be fully implemented), using the growing inequality gap between rich and poor as an indictment of capitalism betrays both a logical fallacy and a misunderstanding of economics. The logical fallacy is the assumption that correlation and causation are the same thing. This misunderstanding of economics assigns to wealth-creating capitalism a zero-sum game model of economics.

A zero-sum game notion can actually be applied to many areas beside economics. All a zero-sum model means is that there is a fixed pool of resources and that when someone gets more, someone else gets less. It's a bit like dividing up a pie—if you get a bigger piece, then the rest of the people splitting the pie get smaller pieces, and the bigger your piece, the smaller everyone else's is—nothing is added (a zero-sum). The underlying assumption is that the size of the pie is fixed and doesn't change.

In *Wall Street*, Gordon Gekko (played by Michael Douglas) believes that business is a zero-sum game when he tells his protégé (played by Charlie Sheen), "Money isn't made or lost; it's simply transferred." When critics of capitalism charge that the wealth of the rich causes the poverty of the poor, they have a view of economics that is much like the family dividing up a pie around the dinner table.

The assumption that the size of the economic pie is fixed is widespread today, but it's not accurate. The zero-sum game view of economic life is probably accurate in parts of the developing world. And it may have been true of economic life in the ancient world, prior to the advent of industrial capitalism.

But capitalism today in the industrial and information economies of the world is not a zero-sum game. In market economies, wealth is not static, but is constantly being created. In fact, every time a profit is made, wealth is created. For example, suppose I have a business that sells shoes that I have imported from another country. I buy the shoes for $5 a pair (which includes all my costs) and sell them for $10. With each pair of shoes I sell, I make a $5 profit. And each time I make that profit, wealth is created, making the size of the pie bigger. Of course, that is multiplied by the millions of profitable transactions that occur regularly, and that suggests that in a dynamic market economy, wealth is constantly being created.

Or take another, more dramatic example. Say my company makes silicon-based computer chips, which have as the basic raw material a resource that is abundant—sand. Whatever I sell my chips for that exceeds my costs, that is my profit and that is wealth being created. My initiative and inventiveness—the use of my human capital—has created wealth out of a formerly useless resource, a great example of the role of human creativity (see chapter 3) in the economy.

Imagine further that my computer chip company, which started out with nothing, now has grown to a company that is worth $100 million. That too is $100 million in wealth that has been created—that didn't exist prior to my company coming on the scene. This means the size of the pie is not fixed at all, but that in a healthy economy, it is constantly growing. It also means that it is possible for everyone to have larger slices of an ever-expanding pie.

It may be that some people get a proportionately bigger slice than others; no doubt that's true. But just because someone gets a bigger share doesn't mean someone else gets a smaller one, or that one person getting a bigger share *causes* someone else to get a smaller one. Just because the gap between rich and poor is growing doesn't mean that the poor are necessarily worse off.

To be sure, there are some parts of the world where the poor are stuck in poverty, where economic life may more closely resemble a zero-sum game. But those are mainly in nations that are not yet participating in the global economy. As we pointed out in chapter 2, though it is true that there are still about three billion left in poverty, global capitalism has been responsible for lifting *the other four billion* out of poverty. Far from capitalism condemning people to poverty, the evidence suggests that it is the most productive way to lift large numbers of people out of permanent poverty. And though it is true that the rich did get richer, it is not the case the poor got poorer.[21]

From 1970–2000, the $1/day poverty rate fell from 20 to 5 percent, and the $2/day poverty rate fell from 44 to 18 percent. The National Bureau of Economic

Research estimates that in those thirty years, close to 500 million people emerged out of poverty.[22] And those statistics come prior to the global growth boom of the early 2000s in China and India, in which far more people entered the middle class for the first time. These statistics also show that the overwhelming majority of the desperately poor are in Africa, in a part of the world where there is little participation in the global economy.

"CAPITALISM LEADS TO OVERCONSUMPTION AND MATERIALISM"

A third critique one hears repeatedly is that capitalism produces a culture that is committed to materialism and consumes much more than it should. Sometimes it is said that capitalism produces a soulless, materialistic culture that leads to spiritual poverty.

For example, preacher and author Jim Wallis writes, "The tree of the American economy is rooted in the toxic soil of unbridled materialism."[23] This echoes the Islamic criticism of the West; as Nafeez Mossaddeq Ahmed puts it, "It's now becoming increasingly obvious that the global political and economic order operates on the basis of a very specific value system rooted in . . . rampant materialism."[24] This critique has some overlap with the earlier criticism that capitalism is based on greed, but the focus of this criticism is more on what capitalism produces—a culture of consumerism with its emphasis on acquisition and defining social worth based on net financial worth.

Let's think about this criticism a bit. It's undeniable that there are lots of materialistic people in capitalist cultures. However, materialism is hardly unique to capitalism. Acquisitiveness, the desire for more, and showing off one's wealth (called "conspicuous consumption") are universal characteristics of human beings, regardless of their culture, ethnicity, or economic system. The reason for this is that like greed, materialism is fundamentally a matter of a person's character (or lack of it), not the economic system in which they participate. Likewise, materialism has flourished in virtually every civilization, even though in some, it was only the handful of very rich who could flaunt their wealth. We think it's naïve to suggest that somehow a change of economic systems will solve what's at the core, a spiritual problem, that emerges in any and all economic arrangements. With respect to the criticism of "materialism," we would argue that materialism is fundamentally a *spiritual* problem, with a spiritual solution.

It is true that the way in which capitalism creates wealth and enables vast numbers to experience upward mobility does allow for more people to be tempted with materialism. But while certainly not extolling materialism, we suspect they would rather wrestle with materialism than experience grinding poverty.

There's no doubt that the wealth-creating capacity of capitalism provides more economic resources to more people. It democratizes materialism, you might say, but that's not the same thing as causing materialism. We must be careful not to equate materialism with the mere having of wealth.

We've already established in chapter 2 that there is nothing intrinsically wrong with wealth, though how you obtained it and how generous you are with it are very important. In addition, we often overlook that the wealth created by capitalism also generates monies for charity, the arts, cultural endeavors, and religious ministries. It enables people to expand their generosity far beyond what they could if they were poor.

"CAPITALISM LEADS TO SIGNIFICANT INEQUALITIES IN WEALTH"

A fourth critique is that "capitalism leads to significant inequalities in wealth." The critics argue that the way wealth is distributed virtually institutionalizes inequality.

Jim Wallis insists that "God hates inequality" and argues that the "great crisis of American democracy is the division of wealth."[25] Michael Moore, in his new film, argues that capitalism has "benefitted the rich and condemned millions to poverty."[26] The real problem is that the inequality is growing. When viewed globally (and more accurately), the contrast is very sharp—between the desperately poor in the developing world and the very wealthy in the developed world.

In responding to this critique, let's be careful about the assumptions that often get "smuggled in" with this criticism. First, there is the assumption that *having a lot is wrong.* Most often, it's religious leaders who raise this point, when they insist that the Bible somehow prohibits accumulating wealth.[27] Nowhere does the Bible make this kind of prohibition As we noted in chapter 2, in biblical times becoming wealthy could involve oppression, theft, or extortion—which the Bible considered fatal compromises of a person's character. It was not the *possession* of wealth per se that was a problem, but the *means* by which it was acquired.

The Bible also condemns wealth without generosity, since the more a person has, the more they are responsible for being open-handed with their wealth. And the Bible condemns dependence on wealth for security and your sense of value—the term reserved for that is *idolatry.*

But there's another assumption that is often hidden in this criticism that capitalism causes inequality, which is that *there's something fundamentally wrong with inequality.* We reject that assumption. Consider the many natural inequalities that we routinely accept. For example, I (Scott) will never be able to play basketball like Michael Jordan did, or swim like Michael Phelps does, because I don't have the physical tools to pull that off. I wasn't born with them, and no matter how hard I worked, I wasn't ever headed for the NBA or the Olympics.

There are inequalities in physical stature, in intelligence, in attractiveness (not everybody can be a supermodel!), and in athletic ability, to name a few. Those inequalities are just a part of the way things are—they may be unfortunate, but they are not necessarily wrong or unfair. Of course, some inequalities are tragic, such as genetic abnormalities that render a person unable to work or care for himself or herself. And the community has the responsibility to care for people who have suffered these kinds of tragedies.

We also accept some inequalities that are the result of a difference in effort, hard work, and diligence. In other words, sometimes there are good reasons for inequalities, when success comes to a person who works very hard, plans well, and saves diligently. Conversely, we feel less sympathy for those who fail to succeed because they are lazy, don't apply themselves, or perhaps dropped out of school and made poor choices about the direction of their lives. Sometimes, people make choices to pursue careers that generally don't make much money but provide great personal satisfaction, such as artists, musicians, actors (only a few hit the big time), and church or nonprofit work. We accept these inequalities, as we do so many others.

However, some inequalities are the result of *injustice*. Those are things to get worked up about. This may be part of the assumption that inequality is wrong—critics may be assuming that all inequality is the result of injustice. But that's not true either, because there is a big difference between inequality of *opportunity* and inequality of *outcome*. That's why it's often helpful to find out what exactly the critic means by inequality.

> **God does not hate inequality, but injustice and oppression.**

When Wallis insists that "God hates inequality," it's not clear where he finds that in the Bible. God does not hate inequality, but injustice and oppression, which both produce and exacerbate inequality. Certainly some inequalities are also unjust. The person who is denied a job or a promotion because of race or gender has been treated unjustly. It's unjust that inner-city children have a substandard education in overcrowded and underfunded schools—that produces an inequality both of opportunity and, usually, of outcome. It's unjust that a person's health insurance company refuses to pay a sizeable hospital bill that they are obligated to pay, forcing that person to lose their home and file for bankruptcy. These are inequalities produced by injustice.

But it's not true to say that all inequality is the result of injustice, or that the inequalities that result from participation in capitalism are unjust. Certainly when people are exploited so that someone else can make a profit, that's wrong, and we have grave problems with human trafficking and a good deal of sweatshop labor that goes on around the world. But we should not equate capitalism with exploitation. Nor is being employed the same thing as being exploited.

Perhaps what troubles the critics of capitalism so much are the *extremes* of wealth and poverty around the world. However, we would suggest that those extremes are far less in the free (relatively speaking) market parts of the world than in regions where the free market is not present. In other words, capitalism has created middle classes virtually everywhere it has been tried. The vast majority of the world's desperately poor are in Africa, where, as we have argued before, market economies are still yet to be widely implemented (or where the conditions necessary for market systems to flourish do not yet exist), and where big-time wealth is often obtained through abuse of political power and corruption. Additionally, the poor in the United States would be considered part of the rich in these other parts of the world, since those who are below the poverty line in the U.S. have many of the consumer items (cars, televisions, refrigerators, cell phones, etc.) and incomes that the poor around the world can only dream of having.

We find it ironic that filmmaker Michael Moore criticizes capitalism as benefiting the rich and condemning millions to poverty. This is because *he is one of the rich whom capitalism has immensely benefited.* Of course, we don't begrudge Moore his opportunity to exercise his entrepreneurial gifts, or his becoming a millionaire. But we would not suggest that his being so wealthy has caused anyone else to be poor, nor are we troubled by the obvious inequality in Moore's wealth and those who don't have as much. In fact, we don't lose much sleep over Moore's, or anyone else's, wealth, because it has not condemned others to poverty (assuming it has been gained legitimately and without exploitation).

BUSINESS CYCLES HAVE
PAINFUL HUMAN COSTS

Ups and downs, booms and busts. An economic history of virtually any capitalist economy will contain examples of both surging economic growth and periods of decline. For example, in recent U.S. history, there was a painful recession in 1979–81 that finally brought inflation under control. This was followed by the boom times of the 1980s, and the bursting of that bubble in the early 1990s. That gave rise to the boom of the later 1990s, followed by the technology stocks (or dot-com) crash of the early 2000s. That further gave rise to the housing boom of the 2000s, followed by the recession that began in 2008.

You can pick any lengthy period of U.S. history and you'll see some examples of these business cycles.[28] When bubbles burst, people get hurt, as jobs are lost and investment values decline. If the slowdown is severe enough, some jobs are lost that never return, and entire industries can actually disappear. These human costs are what Michael Moore had in mind when he accused General Motors of ruining his hometown, throwing people out of work and into homelessness and alcoholism.

Yes, economic slowdowns have human costs. That's why both government and charity exist to help soften the landing for those who lose jobs during those times. But that's not the whole story. Part of the dynamism of capitalism is the way that market forces (especially demand) reallocate resources from unproductive sectors of the economy to productive sectors. Every time there is a new innovation, the market moves resources (capital and labor) to areas in which there is new demand. For ex-

> **Transition and reallocation of resources was a good thing, even though the transfer costs were costly and unsettling.**

ample, when automobiles replaced the horse and buggy, the capital and labor that once went into making the buggy moved to making automobiles. The people who lost their jobs making the buggy (and the entire buggy industry) had to undergo a painful transition to a new job, or new occupation altogether. But overall, we would consider that transition and reallocation of resources to be a good thing, even though there were what were called "transfer costs" that were themselves costly and unsettling.

This has occurred in the telecommunications industry. The telephone replaced the telegraph, telephone answering software has largely replaced receptionists, and the Internet is replacing many different jobs.

More than sixty years ago economist Joseph Schumpeter called this the "creative destruction" of capitalism, when he argued that its ability to move resources according to market demands and innovation provided the engine for its growth.[29]

These transfer costs are real. Yet in our nation they are generally shared by the company, in the form of severance, job training, and placement help; by government, with unemployment insurance; and by the individual, who bears some responsibility for obtaining the training to make himself/herself employable again.

Another part of the story of booms and busts is that sometimes the bubbles are caused by government intervention in the market. Take the housing bubble of the early to mid-2000s. Part of the impetus for this was in the public policy determination as far back as the late 1970s to spread home ownership as broadly as possible. The result was an attempt to bring previously excluded groups into the housing market by making home mortgages more widely available.

This so-called "affordable housing" effort was expanded significantly during the 1990s and early 2000s by a series of inducements to banks and mortgage companies to loosen credit standards, and by the Federal Reserve Board keeping interest rates very low in the aftermath of the 9/11 terrorist attacks. So money was cheap, creditworthiness of borrowers varied widely, and lenders took on more mortgage risk than they had previously. Mortgage originators quickly sold these loans to investors, passing the risk on to someone else. And when the risks that investors took backfired on the banks and their insurers, the government bailed them out. Certainly greed played a major role in the financial crisis of the past few years—but public policy played a major role too. To attribute the boom and crash entirely to capitalism is simply inaccurate.

THE BOTTOM LINE:
CAPITALISM IS *NOT* EVIL

We would agree that there is cause for concern about a capitalism that is entirely unregulated. We don't view the market as the cure-all and end-all of economic life. Likewise, we don't view the market as completely self-correcting —it needs other parts of society and culture to provide some restraints, and we'll spell this out in more detail in chapter 8.

We would further concede that greed is evident in capitalism, but that greed is ultimately a matter of a person's heart/character and can flourish in any economic system. We reject the notion that the prosperity of the rich causes the poverty of the poor. That may have been true in some times and places, but it is not an accurate description of capitalism as a system. We would concede that overconsumption and materialism are evident in capitalist economies, but like greed, materialism is a matter of the heart and hardly unique to modern capitalist systems. We would further concede that there are inequalities in free-market systems, but it's the combination of inequality *and injustice* that is the problem, not inequality by itself.

Finally, we would grant that the transfer costs involved in business cycles are real and affect people's lives, but the responsibility for those costs is shared by business, government, and the individual. Some of the bubbles that are evident in a capitalistic economy are generated by public policy, not economic considerations, and the "creative destruction" of capitalism is also responsible for its dynamism.

Yet with all these concessions, we remain convinced that the economic system of capitalism itself is not evil.

The financial crisis and subsequent recession of the late 2000s have birthed some of the most scathing indictments of capitalism. Understanding the causes of the financial breakdown is critical for ensuring that they are not repeated. In the next chapter we will argue that the financial meltdown was a crisis of the financial system, not of capitalism as a whole. To indict capitalism for the failure of the financial system is to aim one's criticism at the wrong target.

NOTES

1. Although his election in 1998 was open and free, many in the free world believe his rule has become dictatorial. Today, Chavez directly controls numerous business enterprises that were once privately owned, he has turned his nation's military against citizens who disagree with him, and he has seized and shut down media outlets that voice opposition to him. See Charles Hill, *International Business* (New York: McGraw-Hill, 2009), 40–41.

2. Michael Moore, "Goodbye GM," *Huffington Post*, 1 June 2009, http://www.huffingtonpost.com/michael-moore/goodbye-gm_b_209603.html.

3. Martin Sorrell, "The Pendulum Will Swing Back," *Financial Times*, 9 April 2009, 9.

4. Martin Wolf, "Seeds of Its Own Destruction," *Financial Times*, 8 March 2009, 1.

5. See for example, Kevin Phillips, *Bad Money* (New York: Penguin, 2009), 225–29. We'll address this further in chapter 6.

6. Mark 7:20–23.

7. Luke 12:15.

8. Tony Campolo, *Letters to a Young Evangelical* (New York: Basic Books, 2006).

9. Jim Wallis, *God's Politics* (San Francisco: Harper SanFrancisco, 2005), 263, as cited in Jay W. Richards, *Money, Greed, and God* (New York: HarperOne, 2009), 112.

10. Adam Smith, *An Inquiry into the Nature and Causes of the Wealth of Nations* (London: W. Strahan and T. Caddell, 1776).

11. Ayn Rand, *The Virtue of Selfishness* (New York: Signet, 1964).

12. See the further discussion of Rand in chapter 7.

13. *International Comparisons of Charitable Giving* (Kent, U.K.: Charities Aid Foundation, November 2006), as cited in Richards, *Money, Greed, and God*, 123–24. Taxes also correlate inversely with charity. When government takes more taxes, people tend to be less charitable.

14. To read more on this point, see Kenman L. Wong and Scott B. Rae, *Business as Transformational Service* (Downers Grove, Ill.: InterVarsity, 2010).

15. Philippians 2:4.

16. Adam Smith, *The Wealth of Nations*, R. H. Campbell and A. S. Skinner, eds. (1776; repr., Indianapolis: Liberty Classics, 1981), I.ii.2.

17. Baron de Montesquieu, *The Spirit of the Laws* (Crowder, Wark and Paine, 1777), 81, cited in Ruth Chadwick and Doris Schroeder, *Applied Ethics: Critical Concepts in Philosophy*, vol. 5 (New York: Routledge, 2002), 296.

18. Patricia H. Werhane, *Adam Smith and His Legacy for Modern Capitalism* (New York: Oxford Univ. Press, 1991), 108–109.

19. Richard W. Gillett, *The New Globalization* (Cleveland: Pilgrim Press, 2005), 11.

20. As quoted in Richards, *Money, Greed, and God*, 84.

21. Virginia Postrel, "The Rich Get Richer and the Poor Get Poorer—Or Do They?" *New York Times*, 15 August 2002, A1.

22. Xavier Sala-i-Martin, "The Disturbing 'Rise' of Global Inequality," NBER (National Bureau of Economic Research) Working Paper, 8904, April 2002.

23. Jim Wallis, *God's Politics* (New York: HarperCollins, 2006), 263.

24. Nafeez Mossaddeq Ahmed, "Capitalism, Consumerism and Materialism: the Value Crisis." OpEd News, 28 February 2008, at opednews.com.

25. His statement "God hates equality" is taken from Wallis's press conference statement during congressional debate on raising the minimum wage, on 1 February 2007, as reported at huffingtonpost.com. His quotation "the great crisis of American democracy" appears in Wallis, *God's Politics*, 265.

26. Mike Collett-White, "'Capitalism is evil,' Says New Michael Moore Film." Reuters wire service, 6 September 2009, at http://www.reuters.com/article/lifestyleMolt/idUSTRE5850F320090906.

27. Walter L. Owensby, *Economics for Prophets* (Grand Rapids: Eerdmans, 1988), 34–36.

28. For a further discussion on what causes these booms and busts, see Robert J. Barbera, *The Cost of Capitalism* (New York: McGraw-Hill, 2009).

29. See Joseph Schumpeter, *Capitalism, Socialism and Democracy* (1943; repr. New York: Allen and Unwin, 1976).

This crisis serves as a stark reminder of the failures of crony capitalism, and an economic philosophy that sees any regulation at all as unwise and unnecessary.

—BARACK OBAMA, 2008 PRESIDENTIAL CAMPAIGN COMMERCIAL

DID CAPITALISM FAIL
in the
EARLY TWENTY-FIRST CENTURY?

The days of unfettered capitalism are over. " That was the pronouncement I (Scott) heard from an academic colleague one fall day in 2008. Several financial institutions in the United States had just been deemed failures, mostly because of their overexposure to risky subprime mortgage loans. This in turn had touched off the failure of several banks in Europe, while the prices of stocks and commodities began to decline worldwide. Against this backdrop, several countries temporarily closed down their respective stock markets to try and stop massive stock sell-offs, while the entire country of Iceland nearly slipped into bankruptcy.

Those were dark and frightening days, to be sure. Beginning on October 6 of that year, the Dow Jones industrial average closed lower for five out of the next five trading days, amid record-breaking levels of trading volume. And although it was noted at the time that the daily stock market drops were not as severe as those of the 1987 stock market crash, the economic crisis that was unfolding before our eyes was nonetheless unique. Members of both the

House of Representatives and the Senate and presidential candidate Barack Obama called this an economic crisis unlike any since the days of the Great Depression. Given how globalized and interdependent the world had become between the years 1987 and 2008, and the ways in which international markets reacted to the 2008 U.S.-based catastrophe, they were probably right.

No argument for the virtues of capitalism would be honest or complete without addressing the problems that can happen in a free-market economic environment. And in this chapter we'll take a candid and honest look at what transpired within our capitalistic economic system—the good and the bad—during the first decade of this new century. It began with a mild recession in the aftermath of the late 1990s' "tech boom"; was further impaired by the U.S. terrorist attacks of 2001; emerged into a period of tremendous growth and what *seemed to be* an unprecedented level of wealth and prosperity; and then came crashing down in a catastrophe that threatened the entire global financial system.

The "boom and bust" cycle that has defined our nation's economy for the past several years has been painful. As we stated in the last chapter, to some extent the "up and down" cycles are normal in capitalistic economies, and an economic downturn is a necessary and acceptable phenomenon. It allows unproductive enterprises to come to an end, new ventures to begin, and real, genuine economic growth and prosperity to return. Yet the "extreme highs" and "dangerous lows" that have occurred in the U.S. economy thus far this century are unique, and they are worthy of our attention.

CAPITALISM: REGULATED OR WITHOUT LIMITS?

Before we begin examining recent history, we need to reassert an important truth: Capitalism is *not* unregulated or "unfettered." Often when something is perceived to have gone "wrong" in the economy, or something in the economy appears to be "unfair," critics of capitalism will suggest that "unfettered capitalism" is to blame. This seems to happen in both good times and bad, and situations that are far milder than a recession or a global economic meltdown can draw such criticisms.

There's no doubt that injustice can happen in a capitalistic economy. If we are honest, most of us can probably identify specific instances where, for example, individuals were hurt by prices of goods and services that were extraordinarily high (we may think of such situations as instances of "price gouging"), by wages that were extraordinarily low, or by harmful products that were allowed to be placed on the market.

But situations such as these do not necessarily indicate capitalism is inadequately regulated. In fact, situations like these usually don't present an argument against free-market competition at all. Such circumstances instead beg for *more* competition from the free market—more competition among vendors gives them an incentive to lower the prices of their goods and services, and more competition in the labor market gives employers an incentive to pay better wages.

So the notion that capitalism happens without regulation is simply false. Even in the United States, where the free-market economy is still arguably the "most free" of all, enterprise is, generally speaking, subject to significant governmental regulation and oversight. And along with governmental involvement, American enterprise is often subject to the scrutiny of private, nongovernmental watchdog and consumer advocate organizations as well.

The debate over which approach produces the best results—either more governmental regulation of economic activity, or less of it—is a long-standing and legitimate one. But those who attempt to examine the great recession of the early twenty-first century (or any other problem in the economy) and simply blame it on unregulated or "unfettered" capitalism are ignoring the great complexities involved in the crisis, some of which have their origins in faulty regulatory policy itself. Likewise, those who use such rhetoric are usually attempting to argue for more governmental regulation of the economy, yet in the process, they are arguing *against* something that doesn't actually exist.

Having said that, let us also be clear on another important point: Capitalism has not failed, nor did a supposed failure of capitalism bring about the 2008–2009 recession. The crisis was brought about by multiple failures of both the U.S. and global financial systems, and the financial systems are a part of the broader, capitalistic economy. But capitalism itself has not failed. Indeed, capitalism will be the economic system by which Americans, and people around the world, will continue to rebuild.

PART OF "THE SYSTEM"—BUT NOT THE WHOLE

What do you think of when you hear the term "financial system"? When it comes to news about the economy, this term often gets tossed about rather loosely in the media. Sometimes it's used to denote privately owned banks and brokerage firms and hedge funds, and at other times it refers to the United States Federal Reserve, or perhaps even the United States Treasury.

The U.S. financial system includes all of these entities and more. "The system," as such, is an elaborate and interconnected combination of both privately operated and government-run institutions that help to manage, distribute, and invest money, and in some cases regulate the supply of money and interest rates. On an international level, the global financial system would include all of these U.S.-based entities, along with the privately owned banking institutions and investment firms, and the central banks and "finance ministries" of other countries, as well as the International Monetary Fund and the global Bank for International Settlements.

The actual creation and expansion of wealth takes place exclusively in the private sector economy. Entrepreneurs, either utilizing their own money or money belonging to investors, develop new products and services, and seek to produce a "return" on their investment. But at the same time, government-run central banks, the Federal Reserve, and other government regulatory agencies seek to provide order and stability over the supply of money in the economy, the availability of credit, and the procedural functioning of banking institutions. Both private sector institutions and government institutions play a vital role in the functionality of the capitalistic economic system. And if the rest of the economy is doing fine but the financial system is not functioning properly (or vice versa), the overall economic result can still be disastrous.

Problems within the U.S. financial system led to the dramatic economic "boom and bust" cycle of the early twenty-first century. The idea that "problems" would lead to any kind of economic boom may seem strange or counterintuitive (normally we would think of problems as only being associated with negative things, like a downward economic "bust" cycle), but we'll explain shortly how this can happen. For the moment, let's take a look at the conditions of the U.S. economy at the beginning of this century, and consider how the financial system responded to those conditions. As we'll see, the reaction of the financial system to some extraordinary circumstances in the private sector economy was a big part of what began a chaotic and costly period in our nation's economic history.

THE "DOT-COM" BOMB

Anybody old enough to be reading this book is probably old enough to remember something about the so-called "dot-com" craze of the late 1990s and early 2000s. The Internet, originally created by the United States Department of Defense in the 1960s for data communication, gradually became accessible for private, nongovernmental purposes during the 1980s and 1990s. By the mid-90s, personal and popular use of the Internet began to emerge as a mainstream phenomenon in America (especially with the use of e-mail and commercial websites), and this new mode of communicating brought about a transformation of how business happens.

The development of inexpensive and near-instant communication between people all over the world seemingly carried with it the possibility of revolutionizing commerce. Entrepeneurs and investors became starry-eyed at the prospect of selling more goods and services to more people, and even the prospect of developing entirely new goods and services that people would want to purchase.

Nobody would disagree that the Internet has, over time, revolutionized the entire world, including the world of commerce. But unfortunately, in the late 1990s the U.S. economy became dominated by a surge of new Internet-based businesses, many of which were publicly traded on the stock market and whose stock prices soared as investors gorged themselves on the seemingly promising "tech stocks." And during this period, the obsession with web-based commerce was so great that even many traditional, non-web-based businesses found that they could raise the value of their stock simply by launching a website, or by attaching the suffix *.com* (or "dot com") to their business name.

This new "dot-com" craze, where seemingly any business venture that was based on the Internet attracted immediate investor money, was in full swing by 1998. With record levels of cash flooding into the stock market, especially into the technology-heavy NASDAQ, the U.S. economy was, according to some people's analysis, being transformed into something that would be unstoppable with all the new, web-based means of doing business around the world.

The outlook for the new world of "e-commerce" was, to say the least, overly optimistic. And along with this excessive enthusiasm for purchasing stocks in tech companies (then-Federal Reserve Chairman Alan Greenspan would later describe the rapid rise in stock values as a matter of "irrational exuberance"), many of these newly created web-based businesses also operated with their own unique business model.[1] According to the so-called "dot-com theory" of that era, an Internet business's eventual success was based on the company's ability to expand its customer base as rapidly as possible. This belief led many new web-based business operators to spend money with reckless abandon on marketing and advertising, some spending millions of dollars each month, despite the fact that it drove the companies into debt at a dramatic pace.

The dot-com craze, and the economic growth that it stimulated, roared on . . . at least for a while. Because of the surge in the tech sector, the economy began growing so rapidly that the U.S. Federal Reserve was prompted to raise interest rates six times between 1999 and early 2000, in an effort to slow down the economic growth just a bit and to avoid a dramatic spike in consumer prices (inflation). But eventually the promises of "endless growth" in the new online business world were proven to be yet another get-rich-quick scheme. As many of these new businesses consumed all their start-up venture capital, investors began to get nervous and started selling their stocks, and thus, the businesses simply ran out of money and went bankrupt.

The U.S. economy that was red-hot in 1998 was well on its way to a cool-down by 2001. The bursting of the dot-com bubble brought about a $5 trillion loss in market value for technology companies, widespread job losses (especially in computer programming and other "high tech" fields), and a general decline in the overall economy. Some people still lay most of the blame for the burst bubble at the feet of Federal Reserve Chairman Alan Greenspan, because he kept interest rates incredibly low during the dot-com boom days.[2] Yet it is still the case that entrepreneurs and investors alike had been expecting too much, too fast from the new world of online business, and these faulty expectations were significant in bringing about a collapse of these highly overvalued companies and their stocks. In fact, some suggested that the real danger of this period of rapid economic growth was that the assets people were holding, such as these stocks, were so overvalued that when the air came out of the bubble, it was catastrophic for both the individuals who held the stocks and for the companies who placed so much importance on their rising stock price. This is because people borrowed heavily to purchase these stocks, and companies borrowed heavily on the collateral of their stock, so that when the stock prices collapsed, both the individuals who owned them and the companies that borrowed against them were in trouble.[3]

It is true, of course, that in the aftermath of the tech bubble bursting, the Federal Reserve began lowering interest rates so as to increase the availability of credit once again, and to stimulate a slowing economy. But then another, far worse crisis hit the U.S., which prompted another round of interest rates cuts—and this in turn helped bring about an economic "bubble" of a whole new sort.

"9–11" AND ITS AFTERMATH

In the winter of 2001 the U.S. Federal Reserve was well on its way to a steady stream of gradual interest rate reductions. By the time summer arrived that year, the Federal Reserve had cut interest rates 2.5 percent, and by summer's end it appeared that the descending economy had stabilized and had achieved the "soft landing" for which financial system policy experts had been striving, as forecasters began predicting that the U.S. economy would begin growing again in early 2002.

But then the unthinkable happened. On the morning of September 11, 2001, nineteen suicide conspirators from the Al-Qaeda terrorist group hijacked four commercial jets and created mayhem for America and, eventually, the world. Two of the hijacked jetliners were crashed directly into the twin towers of New York's World Trade Center, one was crashed into the U.S.

Pentagon building in Arlington, Virginia, and a fourth crashed in rural Pennsylvania. (Many believe this fourth jet, on a course to Washington, D.C, was intended to hit either the Capitol building or the White House.)

Just under three thousand lives were lost as a result of the 9–11 attacks. This massive destruction of human lives was obviously the greater tragedy brought about that day. Yet at the same time, the beating sustained by the U.S. economy in the aftermath of the attacks was real and tangible, and quickly became painfully evident.

When the U.S. federal government grounded all further commercial air traffic after the hijacked planes crashed, an already struggling airline industry came to a temporary halt. When flight restrictions were eventually lifted, understandably fearful Americans were hesitant to begin flying again, which created further hardship on the airline industry and led to a nearly 20 percent reduction on flights industry-wide. And while Americans were unsure as to when and where another attack might occur, business at restaurants, shopping malls, and other public venues began to plummet.

The New York Stock Exchange, the American Stock Exchange, and NASDAQ never opened on September 11, and remained closed the rest of that week. When they finally did open the following week on September 17, the Dow Jones industrial average set a record for a one-day point decline, falling 684 points, or 7.1 percent. By the end of the week, the Dow had fallen 1,369.7 points, or 14.3 percent, which was at that time the largest one-week decline in history (that record was shattered during the 2008 stock market crash).

So just as the U.S. economy seemed to be ready to grow again after the dot-com chaos, it was hit with the specter of war—what would soon be known as the war on terror. Damages to both New York City and the state of New York exceeded $30 billion and inhibited the exporting sector of the national economy out of New York ports. U.S. stocks lost $1.4 trillion in value, in one week.

With the national economy weakened again and the stock market faltering again, the U.S. Federal Reserve responded with an even more aggressive effort to cut interest rates, to increase the availability of credit, and to stimulate spending.

DOWN, DOWN, DOWN
WITH INTEREST RATES

Beginning on September 17, 2001, yet another effort began to slowly but steadily lower lending rates. On that date, the intended funds rate dropped from 3.5 to 3 percent, and for the next several months the rate declined either a quarter or half a point each time the Federal Reserve Board met, until reaching a "bottom" of 1 percent in June of 2003. This rate remained in place until June of 2004, when, with an economy that was "heating up" quite quickly, the Federal Reserve began yet another slow, steady raising of interest rates. This incredibly low lending rate was a significant part of what led to future problems with adjustable rate mortgages.

Given the Federal Reserve's inclination to lower interest rates in the face of the very crises that we are detailing in this chapter, there have been increasing calls for the Federal Reserve to be abolished altogether.[4] Yet we do not take the position that the Federal Reserve should be abolished. Similarly, it is not our objective here to "second-guess" the Federal Reserve and its officers. Overseeing the monetary policy of the world's largest economy is a daunting task, even under stable circumstances, and navigating this terrain during a time of national crisis is undoubtedly even more overwhelming. In the aftermath of 2001's unprecedented terrorist attacks against America, the governors of the Federal Reserve were acting so as to prevent an economic depression in the United States, and their actions certainly helped to accomplish this.

Our point here is simply that, in terms of monetary policy, the U.S. government's response to two significant and consecutive crises—the dot-com chaos and the U.S. terrorist attacks—was to provide American consumers with easy credit and very low interest rates. That wasn't altogether bad. But for all the good that those policies produced, they were not without negative consequences, primarily creating overvalued assets, this time in housing, as home prices climbed dramatically and out of proportion to reality. And easy credit, along with a confluence of other governmental policies, helped lead to yet another economic crisis, one that eventually became the catastrophe that threatened the global financial system.

REAL ESTATE GONE WILD

"We're creating . . . an ownership society in this country," President George W. Bush announced, "where more Americans than ever will be able to open up their door where they live and say, welcome to my house, welcome to my piece of property."

It was October 2004, just days away from another national election where Bush would end up being reelected to a second term. When the Bush campaign boasted about home ownership being at an all-time high in America, that wasn't just political rhetoric. By the end of 2004, 69 percent of all types of households in America (including both married and single households, and households headed by both men and women) were headed up by individuals who actually owned the dwelling.

In principle, the concept of an "ownership society" is a good one. It encompasses the values of personal responsibility, economic liberty, and the private ownership of property. "Ownership" is completely consistent with the healthy functioning of a capitalist economic system.

It has ramifications beyond merely possessing one's own home, or other material goods. In our culture, we frequently speak of "taking ownership" of something as a matter of "being responsible" or "taking personal responsibility" for that thing, and managing that thing to the best possible ends. Capitalism creates an environment that gives people incentive to assume this kind of responsibility for their own economic needs; for example, their needs for housing, education, health care, or retirement. When people assume this kind of responsibility, it's usually a very good thing.

Yet just because people can buy things with credit doesn't mean that they actually "take ownership" of those things. Similarly, while the U.S. government can make credit easily available, this doesn't mean lenders and borrowers will necessarily behave responsibly with the opportunity.

Within three years the United States emerged from the economic rubble of 9–11 and, in less than three years, re-created a seemingly thriving and growing economy. Yet far too much of that growth was—no pun intended—built on a house of cards.

There's no disputing that within a fairly short period of time after 9–11's devastation, economic indicators in the U.S. had begun to look quite good. While 2002 closed out with the average real gross domestic product growth rate at only 0.3 percent (a dismally low figure, although it is still noteworthy that the U.S. economy grew at all within the first year after 9–11), the real GDP growth rate over the next several years was significant. The posted growth rates for the years 2003 through 2006 were 2.45 percent, 3.1 percent, 4.4 percent, and 3.2 percent, respectively. And during these same years, the average annual unemployment rate remained below 6 percent, reaching a "peak" low point of 4.4 percent in December of 2006.

Those seemed to be "good times" for America, economically speaking. And in many respects they were good times—it's difficult to argue against increasing home ownership and an employment rate of 94 percent or higher. Yet there was some very high-risk behavior that went into the creation of those "good times." For example, while low interest rates stimulated the rate of home purchases, and the increased demand for purchasable homes drove the prices of homes upward, many home owners were able to borrow against the rising equity in their home—usually through the means of a "home equity loan"— and use that borrowed money to purchase other things. This "new money" that people had available to spend as a result of rising home equities also contributed greatly to the overall economic growth of the era. Yet the growth that we're referring to here was dubious, given that it was based largely on borrowed money. In the midst of this economic "boom," there were some warning signs along the way that pointed to potential trouble. And in at least a couple of instances, there is evidence that warning signs were ignored throughout the economy and at the ranks of the federal government.

ABOUT FANNIE AND FREDDIE

Freddie Mac (its official name is the Federal Home Loan Mortgage Corporation) is by definition a government-sponsored enterprise (GSE). Freddie and its counterpart Fannie Mae (the Federal National Mortgage Association) comprise the nation's two largest mortgage finance lenders. And as GSEs, both institutions operate under some unique conditions.

While both companies are owned and operated by private shareholders, they nonetheless enjoy some unique financial protections and support from the U.S. federal government. For example, both "Fannie" and "Freddie" are exempt from state and local income taxes. Both of them are exempt from oversight by the U.S. Securities and Exchange Commission. And both of them have access to credit directly from the U.S. Treasury.

The purpose of these two quasi-governmental entities is to expand the secondary mortgage market (that is, the market for securities and bonds that are "backed" by mortgages) in the United States. As such, they buy individual mortgages, "pool" them together, and sell them to investors as "mortgage-backed securities."

Mortgage-backed securities are themselves very complex financial instruments, wherein the risk of borrowers defaulting on their loans is spread out so as to minimize the pain should defaults happen. When investors buy a mortgage-backed security (MBS), they are essentially backing somebody's mortgage loan, or in other words, the buyers of the MBS become the mortgage lenders (buyers also collect the interest on the loan, as well). This is because an MBS essentially allows a smaller bank to extend a mortgage loan without significant concern as to the borrower's ability to pay back the debt. The loan will eventually be bought by other investors anyway, so the bank becomes merely a "middleman" between the borrower and the broader investment market. We should also note that Freddie Mac and Fannie Mae were not the only lending institutions buying mortgage-backed securities.

One of the main reasons why the MBS (partially consisting of subprime mortgages) became so attractive to banks and investors was that, given the low interest rates and the volatile stock market of the time, banks and investors needed and wanted income investments that produced a decent yield. This, in particular, was what made the subprime mortgage-backed securities so attractive—their rates were quite desirable compared to what banks and investors could achieve more conventionally, and since the risks of default were so spread out, the risks of owning these securities was considered low.

While some have chosen to simply blame "greedy businesspeople" or a "lack of regulation" for the real estate boom-and-bust cycle that led to the great 2008 economic meltdown, that view is essentially inaccurate. Yes, a lack of regulation of the financial system played a part in the crisis, as did risky and selfish behavior among real estate buyers, sellers, and bankers. Yet our government also played a significant role in the crisis.

Consider the role of Freddie and Fannie in the crisis. While the intended agendas of these two institutions may be quite noble and worthwhile, they nonetheless create a scenario where a whole lot of banking and financing power is placed in the hands of politicians. That power can be used as a tool to accomplish the short-term political goals of self-interested politicians, and in the aftermath of the 2008 economic crisis, evidence emerged suggesting that this is part of what happened.

Against this backdrop of financial power in the hands of elected office holders, it's important to consider the agenda of the U.S. government to create so-called affordable housing. This, of course, is not a new phenomenon. The trend toward using governmental means to get "low income Americans" into homeownership took hold during the later years of President Carter's administration, and the trend increased during the years of the Clinton presidency. And while the early twenty-first-century real estate bubble was driven by people from nearly every social and economic class in America, the push to expand affordable housing played a part in both the boom and the bust. Even as far back as 2003, it was noted by the United States Congress that Freddie and Fannie were leading the way with affordable housing efforts.

During the years of the run-up in the housing market, these two GSEs demonstrated a pattern of buying increasing numbers of subprime mortgage loans, those extended to the riskiest and least-qualified borrowers. They did so both because they were considered good investments and because they made additional money available in the mortgage markets. And as Freddie and Fannie went about buying lots of subprime loans, thus making more mortgage capital available to be loaned out, private banks and mortgage lenders were more than happy to initiate increasing numbers of these kinds of loans to risky borrowers. These private lenders knew that they could sell the loan to Fannie or Freddie and make

Private lenders knew that they could sell the loan to Fannie or Freddie and make a quick profit.

a quick profit, so taking risks on poorly qualified borrowers became easy.

Elected politicians make themselves all the more popular, too, if they can make it easier for constituents to buy a house. And there is evidence that to some degree, members of the U.S. Congress ignored signs of potential trouble with Freddie and Fannie, likely because the political upside of people qualifying for mortgages was too good to interrupt.

For example, during a 2003 GSE Reform hearing in the U.S. House of Representatives' Financial Services Committee, Democratic Congressman (and committee chairman) Barney Frank openly described Freddie and Fannie's role in the affordable housing. "Fannie Mae and Freddie Mac have played a very useful role in helping to make housing more affordable," he stated, "a mission that this Congress has given them in return for some of the arrangements which are of some benefit to them to focus on affordable housing." The message from Congress (at least from this committee hearing) to Fannie and Freddie seems pretty clear: keep extending subprime loans to risky borrowers, and we (Congress) will continue to allow your special, government-funded protections and support.

"WE COULDN'T SAY NO TO ANYONE"

In 2003, before the real estate boom took off, the Bush Administration repeatedly attempted to introduce legislation in the Congress that would have strengthened the government's regulation of Fannie and Freddie.[5] Approximately four years later, after the run-up in real estate values and sales, Bush himself proposed "subprime reforms" in 2007, noting an alarming rise in subprime mortgage defaults,[6] but both Democratic and Republican members of Congress refused to support those attempts. At one point in 2005, after Senator Chuck Hagel (R-Nebraska) introduced a GSE reform bill in the Senate, Freddie Mac paid a Republican consulting firm $2 million to help "kill" the bill. As a result, then–Senate Majority Leader Bill Frist (R-Tennessee) never allowed the bill to go to a vote, and it "died."[7]

So while many elected politicians (and a majority in Congress) ignored the possibility of trouble, they weren't alone. In August 2008, evidence emerged indicating that, as far back as 2004, Freddie Mac Chief Executive

Richard Syron had been warned of trouble with his institution, but intentionally chose to ignore it.

According to a report in the August 5, 2008, edition of the *New York Times*, David Andrukonis, the former chief risk officer for Freddie Mac, notified Freddie's chief executive that trouble was on the horizon. In an interview, Andrukonis noted that he had provided Syron with a memo in mid-2004 stating that the company was buying bad loans, loans that "would likely pose an enormous financial and reputational risk to the company and the country." The *Times* report further elaborated that "Mr. Syron received a memo stating that the firm's underwriting standards were becoming shoddier and that the company was becoming exposed to losses, according to Mr. Andrukonis and two others familiar with the document. But as they sat in a conference room, Mr. Syron refused to consider possibilities for reducing Freddie Mac's risks, said Mr. Andrukonis. . . . 'He [Syron] said we couldn't afford to say no to anyone,' . . . Over the next three years, Freddie Mac continued buying riskier loans." Later in 2008, after the housing "bubble" had burst, Syron stated in an interview that "this company has to answer to shareholders, to our regulator and to Congress, and those groups often demand completely contradictory things."[8]

GREEDY LENDERS, GREEDY BORROWERS

The responses by the participants in the real estate crisis varied. Some lenders were greedy and irresponsible, extending mortgages to home buyers who arguably should not have qualified for a loan. Some borrowers were greedy and irresponsible as well, assuming debt that they could not have imagined ever repaying. Some banks went "all in" on mortgage-backed securities, as did some insurance companies by underwriting policies that insured against the default risk of the already risky mortgage-backed securities (the now-famous AIG Insurance Company was one such company). As a result, the financial system, like the failing part in an engine, essentially "seized up," as banks recognized that they were carrying billions of dollars of toxic assets and were near insolvency, and thus severely cut back on their lending to other businesses. And those businesses, dependent on credit for their own ability to make their payrolls and pay their bills, floundered. The "trickle-down effect" was not difficult to see. And if you were a businessperson trying to get a loan at some time in 2008, you understood the problem.

All these various players seem to have been operating with the assumption that real estate values would forever go up, or, at the very least, that they would never drop dramatically. And arguably, the whole scenario was enabled in no small part by two quasi-governmental entities (Fannie and Freddie) that (1) operated with very little regulatory oversight, (2) had the blessing of elected politicians, and (3) unlike commercial and investment banks, were able to borrow directly from the U.S. Treasury.

Describing the intense level of financial activity that surrounded the real estate boom, political and economic commentator Kevin Phillips has compared mortgage expansion to that of the railroads more than a century earlier: "Just as expansion-crazed U.S. and British railroads in the nineteenth century laid pointless track to unwise destinations or overcompeted for markets already well served, in 2004 and 2005 U.S. loan-making standards fell as demand grew." He further notes that the reselling of mortgage loans via mortgage-backed securities "appeared to push risk far enough out the distribution chain to make it [bad debt] somebody else's problem."[9]

Meanwhile new products and services emerged within this sector, which often operated with little or no regulation. "Banks and savings and loan associations had been the big guns through the 1970s, along with insurance companies," Phillips wrote. "Then they lost their old sway before the advance of the expanded forces—mutual funds, nonbank lenders, hedge funds, . . . and others."[10] These new financial products and services have to some degree created an overdependence on the financial services sector for overall growth in the economy, while at the same time expanding financial risk, given how little regulation or supervision surrounds them. Phillips explained that the complexity of many of these new financial instruments, such as derivatives and other asset-backed securities, increased risks. In fact, it was not uncommon for the institutions who held these assets to be confused about even how to value them properly.

NOT HAVING TO PAY FOR YOUR SINS

There's an old adage in business and economic circles that goes something like this: If people are shielded from the consequences of their behavior, then people will be inclined to do some very dangerous things.

Obviously that timeless truth applies to most all of life, and not just to the world of business transactions. But it most certainly applies to the early twenty-first-century real estate "boom and bust"—the reckless behaviors of buyers, sellers, lenders, and politicians that led up to the bust.

This dilemma of people being shielded from the consequences of their behavior is often referred to as "moral hazard," and commentator William Safire once described this phenomenon as "the distortions introduced by the prospect of not having to pay for your sins."[11] In reality, much of the world felt the consequences of the real estate recklessness, inasmuch as it played a major role in bringing about the global economic crisis, so there was really no way to escape the effects of the crisis entirely. But our concern is how the private sector, capitalistic economy is impacted in the long run by the potential "moral hazard" created by government bailouts.

On October 3, 2008, President George W. Bush signed into law the Emergency Economic Stabilization Act of 2008. This bill, first proposed by then–Treasury Secretary Henry Paulson, was the so-called "bailout bill," the piece of legislation that authorized the spending of up to $700 billion U.S. taxpayer dollars to purchase so-called "troubled assets" (bad loans) from lending institutions rocked by what had become known as the subprime mortgage crisis.

Thus TARP (Troubled Assets Relief Program) was born. By extending "financial bailouts" in the form of troubled asset purchases and large cash loans to panic-stricken private banking institutions, the Federal Reserve, the Treasury, and central banks operated by governments around the world likely staved off a far worse economic crisis had they not taken those actions. Even so, the so-called "bailouts," which have been extended under the Obama administration, do raise concerns. For one, the very fact that the federal government has now set the precedent of being willing to rescue banking institutions from their own reckless behavior raises the specter of such behavior continuing. Knowing that government will be there to "break the fall" enables the financial system to continue without facing its own consequences, and thus avoid any meaningful reform.

It also raises concerns about how "free" the free market actually will remain in the future. If private business operators insist on being able to take undue risks with other people's money, businesses will ultimately fall under much closer governmental regulation, and in some cases will likely cease to be privately owned and operated altogether.

NOTES

1. For a description of this period, see Robert Shiller, *Irrational Exuberance*, 2nd ed. (Princeton, N.J.: Princeton Univ. Press, 2009).

2. For more on this, see Peter Hartcher, *Bubble Man: Alan Greenspan and the Missing 7 Trillion Dollars* (New York: W.W. Norton, 2006).

3. In his assessment of the crashes of the early and late 2000s, economist Robert J. Barbera argues that the bubbles were caused by overvalued assets, namely Internet stocks and housing, respectively. See his work *The Cost of Capitalism* (New York: McGraw-Hill, 2009). Economist Robert Shiller advocates something similar regarding asset bubbles in his *Irrational Exuberance*.

4. For an advocate of this position, see Thomas Woods, *Meltdown* (Washington, D.C.: Regnery, 2009).

5. Stephen Labaton, "New Agency Proposed to Oversee Freddie Mac and Fannie Mae," *New York Times*, 11 September 2003, at http://www.nytimes.com/2003/09/11/business/new-agency-proposed-to-oversee-freddie-mac-and-fannie-mae.html.

6. "Bush Proposes Subprime Mortgage Reforms," Associated Press, 31 August 2007, at http://www.foxnews.com/story/0,2933,295369,00.html.

7. "Freddie Mac Arranged Stealth Campaign," Associated Press, 21 October 2008.

8. As quoted in Charles Duhigg, "At Freddie Mac, Chief Discarded Warning Signs," *New York Times*, at http://www.nytimes.com/2008/08/05/business/05freddie.html.

9. Kevin Phillips, *Bad Money* (New York: Penguin Books, 2008), 104–105.

10. Ibid., 107.

11. William Safire, "On Language: Moral Hazard," *New York Times*, 20 December 1998.

I've abandoned free market principles to save the free market system.

—PRESIDENT GEORGE W. BUSH EXPLAINING HIS REASON FOR USING U.S. TAXPAYER DOLLARS TO "BAIL OUT" GENERAL MOTORS AND THE CHRYSLER CORPORATION[1]

GOVERNMENT
INTERVENTION:
HELP *or* HINDRANCE?

Here is a list of terms heard in the halls of the U.S. Congress and mentioned in the media during the waning years of the 2000s: "The "Making Home Affordable" program. The "bank bailout bill." "TARP" funds. "Mortgage asset purchases" and "Cash for Clunkers."

The ways in which Americans communicate about their economy changed considerably during and after the great recession of 2008–2009. In fact, one simply cannot do much reading or talking about the U.S. economy without encountering a bevy of terms and expressions that are now a part of our economic vernacular, yet which mostly didn't exist prior to 2008.

These developments are not merely rhetorical; that is, we're not simply observing the emergence of new phrases and acronyms and technical jargon. Instead, a significant shift has occurred with Americans' attitudes and dispositions toward the economy, and this has led, in part, to changed U.S. public policy regarding the national economy. The result is that the U.S. government (and in some cases state and local governments as well) is becoming far more involved in regulating and controlling the private economic choices and decisions of the citizenry than it has been in many, many decades.

The change in Americans' outlook about the economy is understandable. After nearly three decades of both seemingly incredible growth during the good times and genuine resiliency during down times, it was by any objective measure a frightening experience to observe long-standing banking institutions "suddenly" declaring bankruptcy, while individuals and entire institutions removed assets from the stock market in favor of simple savings and checking accounts, treasury bills, and gold.

The tangible loss in dollar-value to personal investment and retirement portfolios has been astounding as well. According to the *Wall Street Journal*, investors lost an estimated $8.4 trillion of wealth between October 2007 and October 2008.[2] These realities, combined with rising unemployment, quite understandably caused Americans to seek shelter from the storm, along with a new public policy approach to the economy that would hopefully prevent a similar disaster in the future.

So as American individuals and institutions have experienced the pain of the downturn, they have (in many cases quite willingly) become subject to increasing levels of government intervention in what have otherwise been largely private economic endeavors. And as well-intended as this government intervention may be, we believe it is still necessary to question whether the increased intervention is actually helping or hurting.

As we noted in chapter 5, American capitalism is not completely unregulated by the government ("unfettered"), nor should it be (as we'll discuss in chapter 8). Yet we also noted that government policy itself played a significant role in the early twenty-first-century's boom-and-bust cycles and the ways in which government was a contributor to the subprime mortgage crisis.

Given these challenging realities—government oversight and regulation of a capitalistic economy are warranted and necessary, yet the government itself can make the free-market economy worse instead of better—it's essential to question the current shift in economic policy that is underway in the U.S. What has the increase in government intervention in the economy cost, and what has it produced? Have individuals and institutions truly been "stabilized" and set on a new course that will hopefully reduce economic pain and enhance prosperity and stability in the future? Or have they merely been given a "pass," and enabled to continue in their destructive patterns without consequences (i.e., "having to pay for their sins")?

Let's look now at a few of the major public policy efforts that have emerged in response to the "Great Recession," and consider what they have produced thus far.

THROWING THE "TARP"

The scene by September 2008 was distressing: Real estate values were clearly in decline around the country, increasing numbers of consumers could no longer make their monthly mortgage payments (especially as the interest rates on adjustable rate mortgages began to adjust upward), and overall economic productivity appeared to be sinking. At that point, a genuine fear began to set in that banks and lending institutions, many of which were overloaded with real estate–related debt that was not being paid back in a timely fashion, would quit extending credit to other sectors of the economy. If, indeed, lending were to come to a halt, so the reasoning at the time went, the global economy could literally collapse.

On September 24, President George W. Bush spoke to the nation in a prime-time televised address, telling Americans that the entire U.S. economy was in grave danger, and proposing that the federal government supply "urgently needed money so banks and other financial institutions can avoid collapse and resume lending." So serious were the concerns about the economy that on the same day as the president's address, rival presidential candidates John McCain (the Republican nominee) and Barack Obama (the Democratic nominee), in a rare display of political unity, issued a joint statement on the matter.

While McCain's and Obama's respective campaign platforms contained very different long-range fiscal policy proposals, nonetheless both candidates were saying at that moment that the free-market economy was in trouble and needed significant and immediate intervention by the U.S. government. In their joint statement, McCain and Obama agreed that, while President Bush's proposal was "flawed," "the effort to protect the American economy must not fail" and that Congress needed to act quickly.

With the sitting U.S. president and his two would-be successors calling for urgent governmental intervention in what was believed to be a looming disaster, Congress got to work. And while the resulting legislative efforts were complex, the most extraordinary component of the "Emergency Economic Stabilization Act of 2008" was the Troubled Asset Relief Program, also known as TARP.

Under TARP, Congress authorized the U.S. Department of the Treasury to spend up to $700 billion taxpayer dollars to purchase "troubled assets"—loans that borrowers were not paying back in a timely fashion (or in some cases had already been defaulted upon) and mortgage-backed securities (described in chapter 5) from banks and other lending institutions. The goal, of course, was to quickly relieve these lending institutions of the tremendous burden of these bad loans, and thus enable them to begin lending to consumers and businesses again so as to avoid a severe economic shutdown.

While TARP was largely unpopular with the American electorate, many calling it the "bank bailout bill," the president, the Congress, and many in the financial sector of the economy believed that the enormity of the program demonstrated the federal government's good-faith efforts to avert a global economic collapse. Yet from the start, the program was not without risks and concerns of its own.

For one, the program granted an enormous level of decision-making authority over the spending of an enormous amount of U.S. taxpayers' money all to one individual, the secretary of the United States Treasury. And this tremendous concentration of authority over such a large sum of public money quickly led to conflict-of-interest concerns as well. Henry Paulson, the Treasury secretary at the time of the program's inception (and the man who devised the program in the first place), had been the CEO of Goldman Sachs prior to his appointment at the Treasury, and Goldman Sachs was one of the financial firms that potentially stood to benefit from Mr. Paulson's disbursement of the TARP funds. (Goldman Sachs did eventually receive $10 billion of the funds, although the firm paid that money back to the government in early 2009.)[3]

Additionally, there were concerns from the start that the TARP funds would be spent for objectives other than those they were intended for, which was to relieve lending institutions of "troubled assets" and infuse them with liquid assets so they could begin lending again. Those concerns were quickly shown to be legitimate.

Some institutions that accepted TARP funds seemed to have regarded the process as essentially a short-term loan and paid back the funds fairly quickly (as was the case for Goldman Sachs). Although that wasn't precisely the initial intent of the program, it nonetheless seemed appropriate and productive that some private institutions chose to not remain indebted to the government. Yet, less than three months after the program was launched, some of the TARP funds were spent for a purpose that was arguably well outside the scope of the program's intended purposes.

In November 2008, just as Congress was feeling the wrath of Americans who were angered by the "bank bailout bill," executives from the nation's three automakers, General Motors, Chrysler, and Ford, all traveled to Washington to plead their respective cases on Capitol Hill, asking for government assistance (what many regarded as an "auto industry bailout"). Shortly thereafter Ford dropped its request for federal aid, but GM and Chrysler pressed on, insisting that without government help, they would end up in bankruptcy. And while Congress attempted to pass a "financial aid bill" for GM and Chrysler, the legislation failed in the Senate.

Despite the lack of political will on Capitol Hill to provide the car companies with federal financial aid, concerns about the solvency of GM and Chrysler persisted. So, acting quite independently of the Congress, President Bush responded to the cries for help from GM and Chrysler by authorizing the transfer of approximately $13.4 billion of TARP funds to those companies in an effort to help stabilize them.

President Bush's maneuver was regarded as being a violation of the intended purposes of TARP (some even regarded it as being outside the scope of constitutional authority for the president, given that the power to appropriate tax dollars lies with the Congress and not with the executive branch). According to the legislation that established TARP, the category of things that TARP funds could be spent on, troubled assets, was defined rather broadly, yet the kind of institution to which the money could be given—a "financial institution"—was defined quite succinctly and narrowly. Still President Bush approved the federal payments (ultimately the American taxpayers' money) to the two automakers. Similarly, his successor, President Obama, spent TARP funds for nonfinancial institutions after he took office in 2009.

WHERE DID THE TARP FUNDS GO, AND WHAT DID THE PROGRAM ACCOMPLISH?

Conflict-of-interest and program-abuse concerns comprise some of the more obvious dilemmas about the Troubled Asset Relief Program in its early days. Of equal concern to us, however, are these two more far-reaching questions: (1) How are American taxpayer dollars being spent through TARP? and (2) What are these expenditures producing?

In response to the first question, our honest answer is "it depends on who you talk to." In January of 2009, less than three months after TARP's beginnings, a congressional review panel led by Harvard University Law Professor Elizabeth Warren issued a scathing report accusing the U.S. Treasury Department of failing to keep track of how financial institutions were spending the TARP funds.[4] Over the course of 2009, private watchdog groups frequently complained that they could not adequately track TARP fund expenditures, and by September of that year—seven months after President Obama had taken office and his new Treasury Secretary Timothy Geithner had been appointed—members of Congress were still complaining that the Treasury Department was not adequately managing where the TARP funds went and how they were spent.[5]

In terms of what TARP has accomplished, its results are clearly mixed. It is not our desire here to second-guess the Treasury, the president, and Congress in their response to the looming economic shutdown in 2008.

As a general principle that influences our evaluation, we regard it as a destructive thing when government intervenes in the economy and tries to "protect" individuals and businesses from experiencing the effects of their own behavior. Yet we also agree that, insofar as the credit markets could very well have completely "frozen up" during that very challenging period of time in 2008, which in turn could have led to a much worse meltdown, those in our government who were charged with the task of responding to the crisis probably acted as well as they could have. The Troubled Asset Relief Program seems to have helped stabilize the credit markets—indeed, a year after the TARP program was first implemented, America's lenders were no longer in free fall and the financial crisis was in retreat.

That said, we cannot deny that the TARP program has entailed a lot of ambiguity at best, and waste and recklessness at worst. Noting the government's lack of knowledge of how TARP funds were being spent, Congressman Jeff Flake (R-Arizona) remarked in September of 2009 (almost a full year after the program's beginnings), "We know that it [money] was given to the banks and some of the banks have used it to merge with other banks, or acquire other banks. Some tell us they used it to increase lending. Some are rapidly paying it back, some are not. There is some information out there, but I think more is required." At that same time, when asked whether he had concerns about how the TARP program was actually achieving its intended goal of getting banks to lend again, Congressman Barney Frank (D-Massachusetts), the House Financial Services Committee chairman, stated, "Yes, I do think there should have been more pressure at first to increase lending and we still have to do that."[6]

It's also important to note that, despite how President Bush and President Obama believed it was essential to spend TARP funds on "bailing out" GM and Chrysler, both companies ended up in bankruptcy anyway. According to analysis done at the *Chicago Sun Times*, $83.5 billion of Americans' hard-earned tax dollars were given to GM and Chrysler in loans in the months prior to their respective bankruptcy declarations. This suggests that the very costly government intervention and attempts to "save" these companies merely delayed the inevitable (we'll have more to say about government "delaying the inevitable" later in the chapter, as well).[7]

Another consequence of the TARP program, especially given the ways in which TARP funds have been so loosely distributed to such a wide array of companies, is that a substantially larger percentage of otherwise private businesses have become indebted to the U.S. federal government, which in turn has led to the federal government having substantially more control over these private enterprises. It would seem now that the path has been cleared for the government to control such things as the wages and salaries that companies pay.

This kind of governmental control over private business can lead eventually to a form of state-run capitalism.

President Obama has already appointed a corporate compensation czar to help determine what executives should be "allowed" to earn, the types of products and services they provide, and so forth. And in October 2009, President Obama ordered a 50 percent pay cut for the top executives of the banks who were the chief beneficiaries of bailout money.[8] This was after essentially ordering the removal of GM's chief executive officer (Rick Wagoner) earlier that year. This kind of governmental control over private business can lead eventually to a form of state-run capitalism, where government dictates to companies how they will conduct their business.[9]

In analyzing this new reality about the nation's economy, Senator John Thune of South Dakota observed that as a direct result of TARP, the federal government is now a "major owner of more than six hundred U.S. financial institutions and banks, as well as two automakers, an international insurance conglomerate, and numerous other businesses."[10] Senator Thune also noted that this condition places the president of the United States in a position of being a type of "de facto CEO" of very large portions of the economy.

Some may wonder why we would regard this kind of government control over private business to be problematic. Indeed, the notion that "government can't do any worse than corporate America" seems to be a commonly held view. Yet we disagree with this idea for several reasons.

First, the more that economic resources are concentrated in the hands of political figures, the more likely it is that those resources can be used for narrow, short-term political purposes that meet the needs of a very few. (Often the few are the political figures themselves.) There is much precedent for this.

Recall what precapitalist England was like (chapter 3), with the bulk of the nation's wealth concentrated in the hands of a few territorial "lords"; the world of today demonstrates such economic concentrations. Consider, as a more extreme example, the country of North Korea, where the nation's dictator essentially controls all the economic resources that exist in his nation. The dictator, Kim Jong-il, lives a life of luxury (and has the resources to build missiles that currently threaten the U.S.), while the citizens of North Korea struggle with inadequate food, water, and energy supplies.

Such government control of resources contrasts dramatically with the objectives of capitalism. In the free-market economy, all individuals are permitted to own economic resources; resources are intentionally utilized for the broader purposes of creating products and services that are of value to many; investors are allowed the freedom to take risks with their resources with the hope of producing a "return on their investment"; and in this process, sustainable employment opportunities are created.

Of course, the United States government is nowhere near approaching the abuses of North Korean–styled dictatorships. Nonetheless, at times it has exhibited this narrow, shortsighted tendency to use economic resources for very narrow, short-term purposes. Recall from chapter 5 how Fannie Mae and Freddie Mac, two lending agencies that are essentially run by the government, became tools of politicians who seemingly wanted to gain the favor of the electorate by making home ownership "affordable." In the long run these companies that, to use the words of former Freddie Mac CEO Richard Syron, "couldn't say no to anyone," actually helped drive the economy to the brink. Yet these lending agencies did what they did, and their policies were what they were, largely because political figures controlled them.

Another example of government's shortsighted tendencies emerged after General Motors announced its bankruptcy and began a process of corporate "restructuring." GM reviewed how it had been allocating assets, streamlined its operations, and eliminated unproductive elements.

As a part of this process, the company's leaders determined that it was in their long-term financial interest to close a not-so-productive parts distribution plant located in Norton, Massachusetts. General Motors (along with

Chrysler), having been the recipient of billions of dollars of TARP money, was seriously indebted to the U.S. government. Not only that, Congressman and committee chairman Frank had constituents who stood to lose their jobs when General Motors closed their nonproductive plant. So Congressman Frank of Massachusetts intervened. What exactly his intervention entailed is not entirely clear. But eventually, Frank announced that, despite GM leadership determining that the Massachusetts plant needed to be closed, the company had nonetheless agreed to keep the plant open at least for an extra fourteen months. "Keeping this facility open for this extra time gives workers a chance to look at other opportunities," Frank declared, "while at the same time continuing to provide for their families."[11] By every indication, General Motors abandoned—at least temporarily, anyway—part of its plans to restructure and get its own financial house in order, so that it could instead comply with the wishes of a powerful politician.

Generally speaking, government does not use resources as efficiently as do individual citizens and private enterprises.

A second reason to object to the increasing governmental control over the economy is simply this: Generally the government does not use resources as wisely and efficiently as do individual citizens and private enterprises. That may be difficult for some to believe, given all the havoc that private banks, investment firms, and other companies have wrought in recent years. But this is a reality that has been demonstrated repeatedly over the course of history—even fairly recent history.

Consider again some of the examples of government's handling of economic resources that we have examined. General Motors needed to close a plant that was losing money, so as to improve the company's efficiency. But an elected official of the U.S. government got involved in the decision-making process, and the decision in favor of economic efficiency was abandoned. Similarly, the economy of North Korea—which is entirely controlled by the nation's government—produces enough bombs and missiles to pose a threat to the U.S. and Japan, yet it can't distribute adequate food, water, and energy supplies to meet the needs of its citizenry. That's another example of government inefficiency.

The collapse of the former Soviet Union is perhaps the most vivid illustration of government inefficiency in the past century. The Soviet Union was believed at one time to be the shining example of a "centrally planned economy," wherein the government owned all the nation's resources, and governmental officials made all the decisions as to what to do with the resources. Yet, like modern-day North Korea, the Soviet Union produced a military that threatened the free world but couldn't produce adequate food supplies for its own citizens.

Our own U.S. government's inefficient uses of economic resources do not begin and end with the mismanagement of Fannie Mae and Freddie Mac. In the first months after Barack Obama took office, at a time when a new president was charged with leading the nation through an ominous economic downturn, his initial remedy to the crisis—the $787 billion "economic stimulus bill"—drew criticism and concern for its alleged wastefulness. Before passage of the bill, a counterproposal offered by Idaho Congressman Walter Minnick, himself a Democrat, called for a dramatic $650 billion less in governmental spending than the Obama administration's plan. When asked to compare the two bills, Congressman Minnick noted that "the biggest difference is that I've cut out everything that doesn't create jobs."[12] Additionally, eight months after the stimulus bill's passage, the nation's unemployment rate was even worse than what the Obama administration had projected it would be had the stimulus bill not passed in the Congress.[13]

At times the government has seemed unable to track spending under the economic stimulus bill, resulting in complaints from both political parties. The U.S. Recovery Board, created to monitor spending and job creation under the stimulus package, has published inaccurate data regarding the supposed "success" that the bill was creating. On its official website, recovery.gov, the board reports both stimulus spending and stimulus "success stories" in various congressional districts. For example, an expenditure of $761,420 in Arizona's 15th congressional district was reported to have "saved or created" thirty jobs.

The problem, however, is that Arizona's 15th congressional district didn't exist. Additionally, alleged "success stories" were reported to have happened in nonexistent congressional districts in Connecticut, Iowa, and Oklahoma. The government even reported "stimulus success stories" from alleged congressional districts in Puerto Rico, the Virgin Islands, and the Northern Mariana Islands—yet residents in those U.S. territories have no representation in the U.S. Congress, and thus, no congressional districts exist at all in those regions.[14]

Such poor management and reporting of government spending caused the Democratic chairman of the House Appropriations Committee to assail his own party's administration: "The inaccuracies on recovery.gov that have come to light are outrageous," declared Congressman David Obey, "and the Administration owes itself, the Congress, and every American a commitment to work night and day to correct the ludicrous mistakes."[15]

Just as it was with the TARP program, federal authorities struggled to accurately answer "Where did the stimulus money go?" This apparently reckless disbursement of hundreds of billions of TARP dollars, along with the funding and manipulation of Freddie Mac and Fannie Mae—all at the expense of the American taxpayer—demonstrates this reality of government inefficiency.

With this in mind, let's examine yet another way in which our government has responded to the severe economic downturn, and then consider what those efforts have produced.

FROM "AFFORDABLE HOUSING" TO "RESCUING MORTGAGES"

Nobody is well-served by losing their home, right?

That may seem like a noble and just assumption. It might even seem like the "compassionate" position to take, in the face of somebody who is genuinely threatened with the loss of a house. But in the midst of a painful real estate bust, complete with its staggering increases in home foreclosure rates, the notion of preventing home losses became more than just a compassionate idea. It became a matter of federal policy as the government intervened in the free market once more to try to curtail foreclosures.

The problem of skyrocketing home foreclosures was in no small part brought about by the resetting of adjustable rate mortgages (as we mentioned earlier in this chapter). As the lending rates of these mortgages adjusted upward over time—just as they were designed to do—monthly payments on those mortgages became more expensive, and many borrowers found that they could no longer afford to make their monthly payments. Some of these borrowers were actually speculators who simply walked away from their mortgages when they could no longer make the payments, especially since in many cases what they owed on the home exceeded its value. In March 2009, President Obama announced the "Making Home Affordable" initiatives, a set of federal policies budgeted to cost $75 billion in TARP funds, and intended to help make it "easier" for home owners to remain in their homes and to continue paying on their mortgages.[16]

The effort itself was complex and was formulated with both federal guidelines and guidelines to be established by each of the individual fifty states. The effort also proved to be so confusing that about six months after the program's inception, Freddie Mac (one of the lenders that was offering the so-called affordability assistance to *some* of its borrowers) actually hired a private firm to send trained professionals door-to-door in certain regions of the country to explain to home owners how the program worked.[17]

The objective of "Making Home Affordable"—reducing monthly mortgage bills so borrowers would presumably keep paying on their mortgages—was to be accomplished on a case-by-case basis, and by a variety of means. This included lowering the interest rate of the loan (to as low as 2 percent in some cases); reducing the principle on the loan; and extending the term of the loan, in some cases to a maximum of forty years. The government stipulated that, for certain qualified mortgage holders, loans that were held by the government-controlled Freddie Mac and Fannie Mae would be refinanced or otherwise "modified" to provide the borrower with more manageable monthly terms. Not surprisingly, the government was also able to some degree to get lenders who accepted "bailout funds" to follow suit and agree to begin modifying the loans of their struggling clients as well (even though to do so meant that these lenders would be working against their own interests and forgoing revenues they were clearly entitled to be earning).

Given the many ways in which home foreclosures were negatively impacting the entire economy, it seemed to some like an idea that would be beneficial for everyone. But as is so often the case when the government intervenes in the free market, the results produced by the "Making Home Affordable" initiatives have been, as of this writing (almost one year later), less than desirable.

A recent report issued by federal bank regulators indicated that, among home owners who fell behind on their payments and were offered help with their mortgage through the "Making Home Affordable" program (in the form of a "loan modification"), more than 50 percent ended up falling behind in their payments again.[18] Thus, it seems that the government's best effort to "save" people from losing their home helped give rise to a whole new problem—the phenomenon of "redefaults."

From our vantage point, we wonder if the "Making Home Affordable" program has actually helped individual consumers and the country as a whole, or if, possibly, it has made matters worse. The government's effort to give mortgage borrowers a "break" with their financial commitments may very well slow the rate of loan defaults in the short run, and thus help stave off the dramatic decline in home values. But if borrowers who are "assisted" by this program do not make wiser, more prudent choices in the future, we could see the problem of redefaults continue or perhaps get worse, while private lenders and American taxpayers bear the risks and the costs of the program.

And while we wonder about the net effects of the program, we certainly believe that this instance of government intervention has brought about further concerns of "moral hazard." Indeed, it would seem that at least some of the individuals who have had their mortgage loans "modified" in one fashion or another have been allowed to "not pay for their sins"—that is, they have been allowed to escape the results of their own poor choices of assuming too much debt and agreeing to financial commitments that they could not keep.

We also believe this program raises concerns about fundamental fairness in the finance market. Easier, more palatable financing terms are being offered to people who, for whatever reason, have *not* acted responsibly with their existing financial commitments. Conversely, borrowers who have continued to earn sufficient income in the midst of a recession and have been responsible to make their mortgage payments in a timely fashion, regardless of how much of a sacrifice those house payments may cost, remain ineligible for the more favorable financing terms. This amounts to the government rewarding bad behavior. And rewarding bad behavior generally ensures more bad behavior, not good behavior, in the future.

PRIVATE PROPERTY AND PUBLIC HOUSING

"You just don't know what it's like where I live." I (Austin) was fifteen years old the first time somebody said those words to me. I'm still not sure to this day what exactly that remark was intended to convey, but at the time I was left feeling guilty and ashamed. Yet the remark led to one of the greatest economics lessons that anyone could hope to experience.

At that time, my involvement with a church-based youth group in my suburban southern California hometown of Huntington Beach had led me to some interaction with a youth group from the inner-city region of nearby Long Beach. Over time, the kids from Long Beach began to speak of their life in "the projects"—the federally funded housing project in which they were living—and they spoke begrudgingly of the broken-down conditions of their individual apartments.

After hearing repeatedly about how terrible life was in "the projects," I offered to join the kids in Long Beach for a weekend and assist in some neighborhood cleanup and repair work.

I'm glad I visited and could offer help, but I wasn't prepared for what I would encounter. Bedroom doors that had been kicked in. Light fixtures that had been smashed. A kitchen wall was defaced with graffiti. The apartments were being vandalized, yes, but they were being vandalized *from the inside.* Some (but not all) of the residents, themselves, were damaging their own homes, homes that the government had provided for little or no cost to them.

I'm not suggesting that all who live in public housing are irresponsible or ungrateful, or that poverty is always self-inflicted. The story does, however, illustrate a very important economic truth, a truth we alluded to earlier, about the significance of property ownership.

When an individual truly owns a particular item—and by "owns" we mean that the individual has incurred a personal cost in acquiring the item—then that person has an incentive to treat the item well and to manage it effectively. If, on the other hand, a person possesses something that was given to them at little or no cost, then, generally speaking, the person does not have as much of an incentive to properly care for that item. Private property ownership (and by "property" we mean any material good or resource) can, thus, empower individuals to act responsibly with resources, whereas the absence of private ownership encourages irresponsibility and being wasteful with resources, as renters know they won't incur any direct, personal consequences for their actions.

If you don't think this phenomenon of private property ownership is that significant, then consider this simple question: How do you treat a rental car or a hotel room, as compared with your own car or home? Rarely do people clean their rental cars and hotel rooms, because they have no incentive to do so. But, conversely, most of us are motivated to clean our own cars and homes (or to pay somebody else to do these things) because if we don't, we directly experience the consequences of our behavior.

Similarly, anyone who has done effective work with the poor and impoverished knows that simply giving material resources to a needy person does not necessarily "solve" their problem. The successful and widely respected Habitat for Humanity charity home-building organization exemplifies a wiser and more prudent approach to helping the poor, while at the same time recognizing and respecting the significance of private property ownership. When selecting a candidate for whom they will build a home, the organization considers the candidate's willingness to participate in the home-building process, and the candidate's likely ability to pay back the cost of the home.

The significance of private property ownership is also the reason why we can say that, generally speaking, government does not manage material resources as effectively as private individuals and organizations. When government owns something, that thing is no longer owned by private individuals or groups, but rather, it is, by definition, a matter of "collective" or "public" ownership. When, for example, the federal government possesses a sum of money that has been collected from multiple individuals in taxes, that money is then considered "public money"; it is essentially owned by "everyone" who pays federal taxes.

The incentive to responsibly manage public resources is significantly less than the incentive to manage one's own resources. When "everyone" owns something, then, in effect, no one owns it, because no one individual or group will directly experience the consequences of that resource being mismanaged or wasted.

This is why governmental officials quite naturally have a tendency to misuse public money. It's not their own, personal money, and if it gets lost or wasted, they won't necessarily feel the direct effect of that loss. In a sense, it is simply "too easy" to be reckless with public money. The examples of corporate bailout programs and mortgage relief programs that we've examined illustrate this dilemma quite effectively.

THE WAY FORWARD

So if more government control over the private economy and a system of "state-run capitalism" are not the keys to a more prosperous future, then what is? Well, for one, the future success of our capitalistic economy will require that our government demonstrate a healthier respect for the significance of private property.

We'll have much more to say about this important concept in chapter 8, where we detail certain limits on the market. But, just as we've discovered here in this chapter, the reality of private property ownership can create incentives for people to act responsibly with economic resources, while at the same time motivating them to impose limits on their own behavior, in particular, limits on the levels of risk and debt they are willing to assume. As a result, private property ownership can encourage sensible behavior, in ways that government programs and regulations do not, and public servants in our government must begin to recognize this.

Another essential ingredient for our future success will be for government to respect the freedom of individuals and groups to succeed, but also, to fail. As economist John Tamny has noted, businesses will not be incentivized to behave more responsibly because government sets limits on executive salaries (as the Obama administration is doing). Businesses will, however, be incentivized by the power of ownership. If they can fully own their successes without having punishing tax rates or government-imposed limits, they will have incentive to create more success, and if they are left to fully own their failures (rather than rely on government for a "bailout"), they will have an incentive to learn from their mistakes and avoid future failures.

These principles apply to businesses large and small, but they apply to individuals as well.[19] Yet, if our government continues ignoring these principles, creating an environment for "moral hazard" and rewarding bad behavior with a "bailout," it most certainly will create more bad behavior, and more economic destruction, in the future.

As we've stated throughout this book, we do not envision a free-market economic system that is devoid of any government regulation, and we likewise do not desire a society that is coldhearted to the poor and needy. But we also recognize that government's best attempts to "save" people from crises can, themselves, be wasteful, and can actually make problems worse. In order for our economy to thrive—and in order for capitalism to fulfill its potential—the proper mechanisms must be in place that give individuals incentives to make better choices for themselves.

NOTES

1. Then-President George W. Bush in a CNN interview with Candy Crowley, 16 December 2008.

2. Betsy Stark, "The Stock Market Crash of 2008," *ABC News*, 10 October 2008, http://blogs.abcnews.com/moneybeat/2008/10/the-stock-marke.html.

3. Christine Harper and Elizabeth Hester, "Goldman Sachs Said to Be in Talks to Repay TARP Funds," *Bloomberg News*, 24 March 2009, http://www.bloomberg.com/apps/news?pid=20601087&sid=aIezubwp9xFE&refer=home.

4. Daniel Arnell and Alice Gomstyn, "Where Did Taxpayer Money Go? Panel Slams Treasury," *ABC News*, 9 January 2009, http://abcnews.go.com/Business/Economy/Story?id=6606296&page=1.

5. Manuel Quinones, "Lawmakers Question How TARP Money Was Spent," Public Radio International, 17 September 2009, http://www.pri.org/politics-society/government/how-tarp-money-was-spent1613.html.

6. Ibid.

7. Ibid. See also Sandra Guy, "Where Did Our Billions Go?" *Chicago Sun Times*, 3 October 2009, http://www.suntimes.com/technology/1804718,CST-NWS-TARP04.article.

8. Jim Puzzanghera and Walter Hamilton, "Obama to Cut Execs' Pay 50%," *Los Angeles Times*, 22 October 2009, A1, http://www.latimes.com/business/la-fi-executive-pay22-2009oct22,0,3885122.story.

9. For discussion of what a state-run capitalist system might look like, see Kevin Phillips, *Bad Money: Reckless Finance, Failed Politics, and the Global Crisis of American Capitalism* (New York: Penguin, 2008).

10. John Thune, "Time for a TARP Exit Strategy," *Wall Street Journal*, 4 October 2009, http://online.wsj.com/article/SB10001424052748704471504574447122027550500.html.

11. John Moroney, "Barney Frank Helps Delay Closing of GM Plant," NECM.com, 4 June 2009, http://www.necn.com/Boston/Business/2009/06/04/Barney-Frank-helps-delay/1244165040.html.

12. Greg Meyer, "Minnick Has His Own Stimulus Proposal," KLEW-TV, 6 February 2009, http://www.klewtv.com/news/39170247.html.

13. Ross Douthat, "Off the Chart," *New York Times*, 15 November 2009, http://www.nytimes.com/2009/11/16/opinion/16douthat.html?_r=1&ref=opinion.

14. Jonathan Karl, "Jobs 'Saved or Created' in Districts That Don't Exist," ABC News, 16 November 2009, http://abcnews.go.com/Politics/jobs-saved-created-congressional-districts-exist/story?id=9097853.

15. Ibid.

16. Stephanie Armour, "Some Mortgage Modifications Push Payments Higher," *USA Today*, 15 September 2009, as cited at http://www.azcentral.com/business/realestate/articles/2009/09/15/20090915mortgagemods.html.

17. E. Scott Reckard, "Knock, Knock, Who's There? Freddie . . . ," *Los Angeles Times*, 29 September 2009, at http://latimesblogs.latimes.com/laland/2009/09/freddie-mac-mortgage-loan-modification.html.

18. "Homeowners in Financial Trouble Often Redefault," Associated Press, 30 September 2009, http://www.azcentral.com/business/realestate/articles/2009/09/30/20090930redefault.html.

19. John Tamny, "Banker Pay Curbs Won't Work," *Orange County Register*, 25 September 2009, http://www.ocregister.com/opinion/pag-212522-firms-financial.html.

My attitude is that if the economy's good for folks from the bottom up, it's going to be good for everybody. I think when you spread the wealth around, it's good for everybody.

—BARACK OBAMA, CAMPAIGNING FOR THE PRESIDENCY IN OHIO[1]

CORPORATE GREED
and the
POLITICS OF ENVY

When individuals in a free-market economy break the rules, the repercussions can harm many people. Elected public-policy makers, who have a natural inclination to want to intervene in private affairs, often end up interfering with the free market and overreacting to the "rule breakers" with destructive laws and regulations.

Consider this: What is the first thing that comes to mind when you hear the names Enron, Bernard Madoff, Countrywide Financial, and Peregrine Systems?

Each of these names has been associated with one type or another of American business. Three of them you have probably heard of before (one of them you may not have). All four of them hold a distinct place in the history of American enterprise. And each one of them has been a part of a long list of American business scandals, all of which have happened within the first decade of this new century.

First, let's consider the company that may be the least familiar. Peregrine

Systems was a software company begun in 1981 by five individual "founder/employees." During the 1980s the company grew its product line rapidly, both by developing its own products and by acquiring the creations of other, smaller companies. The original founders eventually sold the business to another company, yet the business retained the Peregrine name and continued to grow. By 2000, Peregrine had achieved market domination in several select areas of software development, and in 2005 the company was itself acquired by the much larger Hewlett-Packard Company.

Sounds like a great story. Five entrepreneurial people decide to take the risk of "going into business for themselves" and seize the opportunities emerging at the dawn of the computer age. Their products become so well received around the world that another company comes along and offers to buy the business. The new owners, in turn, take Peregrine to even greater heights, and eventually the company ends up in the hands of a corporate conglomerate. Entrepreneurs working hard, producing great products and services, and creating innovations along their pathways to success.

It sounds like another great story of achievement, enabled by American capitalism. But something happened on the way up. In May 2002, Peregrine Systems was hit with a damaging accounting scandal. The company was eventually accused of falsifying sales and exaggerating revenues in excess of $100 million. Peregrine ended up laying off almost half of its workforce, and entire divisions of the company were sold in order to retain enough money to survive, as the company filed for Chapter 11 protection. By 2003, the United States Securities and Exchange Commission (SEC) had begun to investigate, and the investigation eventually led to the indictments of eleven senior managers, none of whom were the original founders of the company. By the time Hewlett-Packard was ready to buy the company, Peregrine was willing to sell for just slightly more than two times company revenues (a very slim margin, given the company's previous potential). It wasn't such a great story of success after all.

Peregrine Systems is not the only recent company in America that started well and ended badly. Begun in 1969 by business partners David Loeb and Angelo Mozilo, Countrywide Financial had rather humble beginnings and struggled at first. But hard work and diligence paid off, as Countrywide became so profitable that in 2003 it was labeled as the "23,000% stock" (the company was publicly traded and produced a high yield for its shareholders).[2]

After reaching tremendous heights, Countrywide hit bottom. By 2007, it was clear that the lender was in too deep with the "affordable housing" push by Freddie Mac and Fannie Mae, and was caught in the tailspin of the subprime mortgage crisis. Worse still, Countrywide got caught in what was to become known as the "friends of Angelo" scandal ("friends" of cofounder Angelo Mozilo), wherein members of Congress were allegedly given mortgage financing at below market financing rates.[3] In January 2008, Countrywide announced that it was being taken over by Bank of America in order to avoid bankruptcy; six months later Bank of America acquired Countrywide. In October 2008 Countrywide agreed to pay up to $8.68 billion of home loan and foreclosure relief to settle charges in eleven states of misrepresenting loan terms, loan payment increases, and borrowers' ability to afford loans.[4]

SOMEBODY'S GREED, OR SOMEBODY ELSE'S ENVY?

Have no doubt—when participants in our economy cheat, people get hurt. Sometimes the cheaters themselves get hurt. Sometimes the people surrounding the cheaters (employees, associates, family, friends, and so forth) get hurt. And sometimes, "all of the above" get hurt.

Notice the pain and suffering associated with the Peregrine case. Lots of employees lost their jobs when the scandal hit (we can also imagine that those who remained employed at Peregrine were left to work in a very tenuous, stressful environment). Stakeholders in the company lost money and opportunity. Families and friendships were no doubt damaged. Individual lives, careers, and reputations were destroyed.

It's not a huge leap to presume that at some point during the history of Peregrine Systems, certain individuals became greedy, and their greed motivated them to do just about anything; obviously they became willing to break the law in order to accumulate more wealth and "success." It's a sad state of affairs when people lose the discernment and self-control required to act responsibly, and instead choose to act recklessly in pursuit of their own am-bitions, without regard for how their actions may affect others. But when people are free to make choices, sometimes they make bad choices.

Before we go further, it's important for us to convey clearly what we are re-ferring to in this chapter as it pertains to "greed." In chapter 4, we noted that greed is often invoked when people want to criticize capitalism. We also noted how Adam Smith, the ideological founder of capitalism, addressed this no-tion of greed in his works.

For the purposes of our discussion in this chapter, we are regarding greed as a negative thing. We want to make this clear, because it is often the case that in discussions of capitalism and contemporary business ethics, some people like to cling to the notion that "greed is good." In principle, we don't agree with this at all.

Yet as we examined earlier in chapter 4, every human being quite naturally and normally functions with a level of self-interest. This is generally healthy and good. We considered how self-interest rightly impacts our economic choices. Many of Ayn Rand's philosophical writings contributed greatly to our understanding of how self-interest motivates one to achieve and to succeed, and how, in turn, one's success and achievements can produce benefits for others.[5] We would contend that while self-interest can be a productive moti-vator, greed is a destructive motivator. Unlike self-interest, greed can lead people to become so ruthless and reckless that they actually do harm to their own interests, and to the interests of others as well. The case of Peregrine Sys-tems illustrates this quite effectively.

There's another way in which greed and self-interest are misunderstood. Sometimes people will use the term *greedy* to describe the rational, self-interested economic choices made by others, simply because people don't like the choices made by others. In this case, *greed* or *greedy* is intended to be a pe-jorative and judgmental description, but such descriptions many not neces-sarily be grounded in the facts.

Think of it this way. When business executives receive multimillion-dollar salaries or earn hefty bonuses, they're likely to be labeled by some as "greedy." There is little regard for what the business person in question had to accomplish in order to achieve their earnings: his or her training and education, the level of profit the executive needed to produce for the business, and the level of assets the executive managed. Some will simply observe one individual making a lot of money and then conclude that the executive is earning too much and is necessarily motivated by greed.

The same kind of accusations are often made toward entire organizations. Sometimes when a corporation lays off employees or cuts salaries, it is labeled as greedy for doing so. Worse yet, when a company eliminates jobs in the United States and outsources those positions to other countries (presumably to countries where workers can be employed for lower wages), that also qualifies as greedy in the minds of some. There may be no consideration for the pending struggles within an organization that led to the cutbacks, and there may be no regard for the confounding public policies (exorbitant tax rates, or excessive governmental regulation of the business) that make it unaffordable to do business in a particular region. Some critics are quick to look at the achievements and decisions of other individuals and organizations, and cry "greed."

Another reality often overlooked by people who are quick to allege corporate greed is the fact that publicly traded corporations assume a delicate combination of needs and obligations. While job cuts or facility closures can cause pain and may seem on the surface like ruthless choices that merely benefit "greedy executives," they can be necessary decisions to benefit the stockholders of a company.

Ultimately, the owners of a publicly traded company are the stockholders —individual people who assume the risk of putting their hard-earned money in the hands of business executives in exchange for the possibility of earning a return on their investment. And given the large percentage of the American population who own stocks, decisions that benefit the bottom line of publicly traded companies also benefit the "bottom line" of many individual, everyday private citizens. Put another way (and to use a couple of common, contemporary metaphors), the needs and interests of Wall Street often intersect those of Main Street.

Thus, just because individuals make lots of money or companies make unpopular decisions, doesn't necessarily mean that those individuals and organizations are motivated by "greed." But here's another thought to ponder: Perhaps, at times, those who claim greed are, themselves, reacting to a situation out of a sense of envy.

Here is a set of definitions to help distinguish between the two motives. *Greed* is "excessive desire, especially for wealth," according to the American Century Dictionary; it defines *envy* as "discontent aroused by another's gains, successes, etc."

Capitalism can enable the creation of wealth for increasing numbers of people. . . . Because of this, capitalism can help to diminish the problem of envy.

As we noted in chapter 4, envy can often be greater in environments where there is no opportunity for upward mobility. We also noted that the Bible indicates the opposite of contentment is envy, not ambition.

Capitalism has transformed the world with its ability to enable the creation of wealth for increasing numbers of people and to extend economic opportunity to people regardless of their upbringing, ethnicity, or family lineage. Because of this, capitalism can help to diminish the problem of envy among societies.

Yet, despite the success of capitalism, human nature remains imperfect, and people still become envious. Just as it is unacceptable and unhealthy for a society to become indifferent toward its poorest and weakest members, so also is it unhealthy and unacceptable for a society to be motivated by a sense of envy toward its wealthiest members. In fact, it is socially destructive when individuals become so discontented with their own circumstances that they allow themselves to act out of a sense of envy toward those who seem to live in better circumstances. This can result in American public policy that seeks to take away increasing amounts of wealth from highly successful people and organizations. Such policies, at times, seem to be motivated by a sense of "envy" and a desire to "get back" at those who "have too much," and why punitive economic policy rarely produces success for anybody. Later in the chapter we will look at some examples of such public-policy decisions.

But first, let's look at another scenario in which participants in the free-market economy cheated, seemingly motivated by destructive greed—and how a very burdensome law resulted from the cheating.

REAL GREED—WHAT WENT WRONG?

This company once employed approximately 22,000 people from around the globe. It led the world in the electricity, communications, pulp and paper, and natural gas industries, while it also participated in the plastics, metals, steel, and freight industries (among others). For six consecutive years, from 1996 to 2001, *Fortune* magazine named it the "Most Innovative Company in America." In the year 2000, it allegedly produced revenues of over $100 billion.

Yet by the middle of November 2001 it began one of the most complex, and at the time, the largest, bankruptcy proceedings in history. Today, the very name of the company is synonymous with the concept of corporate scandal.

We're describing the Enron Corporation. And not only did the Enron scandal signal the largest failure of an American business at the time, it also stands today as the largest auditing failure in history. The accounting and consulting firm of Arthur Andersen, at the time one of the world's Big Five accounting firms with a heritage dating back to 1913, was indicted and convicted in 2002 of criminal charges relating to its handling of the accounting affairs of Enron.

After the conviction was handed down, the Arthur Andersen firm surrendered its licenses to practice as certified public accountants in the United States, given that the SEC does not allow convicted felons to audit public companies. This resulted in the firm losing both its American clientele and its overseas business, fallout from the damage done to its reputation. The U.S. Supreme Court actually reversed the conviction of Arthur Andersen in 2005, but the company has never returned to its former prestige or profitability.

All told, the scandal brought about twenty-three criminal convictions. (Sixteen individuals pled guilty to crimes committed at Enron, while seven other individuals, including Enron's former chairman of the board, Kenneth Lay, and former chief executive officer Jeffrey Skilling, were tried and convicted.) Enron stockholders are estimated to have lost $11 billion in wealth, based on the stock's "high" value of $90.00 per share and its eventual decline to "worthless" status. For many Enron employees, the loss in the company's stock value meant the loss of their life savings as well. (Sadly, while these employees were locked out of selling the stock during its downward spiral, company executives were cashing in their shares.)

Three people associated with the scandal lost their lives (Kenneth Lay died of a heart attack days before his sentencing; Neil Coulbeck, a banker living in England who was set to be extradited to the U.S. as a potential witness in the Enron scandal, turned up dead in a public park in London just before his extradition—his death was eventually ruled a suicide; and former Enron executive Cliff Baxter was also believed to have committed suicide). And it is estimated that between the demise of the Enron Corporation and the Arthur Andersen firm, over 100,000 individuals worldwide lost their jobs. As we said earlier, when individual participants in our economy break the rules, lots of people get hurt.

The history of the Enron Corporation traces back to 1932, to what was then known as the Northern Natural Gas Company of Omaha, Nebraska. Northern Natural Gas was eventually acquired by the Internorth Holding Company in 1979, and by 1985, Internorth was merged with Houston Natural Gas to form the newly founded Enron Corporation. In its early stages, Enron and the entities of which it was comprised seemed to symbolize the best of American capitalism and free-market enterprise. And given its public track record, it was not surprising that Enron was repeatedly labeled as the "Most Innovative Company in America."

Given his reputation of integrity and honesty, Arthur Andersen likely would have been horrified at how his company met its demise.

The history of the Arthur Andersen accounting and consulting firm is equally as impressive, if not more so. Arthur Edward Andersen, the founder of the company, was known as an extraordinary person, and in many ways his life exemplified the transformative capacity of American capitalistic enterprise. Born in 1885 and orphaned at the age of sixteen, Andersen began working to support himself by day and went to school at night. After beginning his accounting business in 1913, he continued to attend school and eventually completed his bachelor's degree in business in 1917. Not only did he grow his business into one of the world's largest accounting firms, Andersen also developed innovative accounting systems and training programs, and was a charitable supporter of educational institutions, serving terms on the Northwestern University Board of Trustees, and as the university's president. He died in 1947, and given his reputation of integrity and honesty, he likely would have been horrified at the way in which his company met its demise.

So what went wrong with Enron and Arthur Andersen? Some point out that Enron's management team was heavily compensated with the issuing of stock options. Such options are a very common form of noncash compensation that many companies offer their employees, especially executive-level employees; Enron was by no means unique in this regard. As a practice, offering stock options to employees can be an effective way for a company to pay its staffers, without depleting the company of immediate capital resources. Theoretically, it is also a way for a company to give employees an incentive to behave in ways that will boost the company's stock price; the more the company's employees produce, the higher the stock value rises, and thus, the more wealth created for the employees.

Giving employees an incentive to perform by issuing stock options is fine, as long as everybody works hard, plays by the rules, and remains productive. So how can stock options be bad? The answer: Some of the recipients of stock options are so eager to "cash in" that they cheat and deceive in order to raise the stock price higher than its actual value. That, in a nutshell, is what happened to Enron. And the route to deception was very circuitous, complex, and confusing —so confusing, in fact, that it's still not clear today if Enron's lawyers and accountants completely understood everything that was going on in the company.

In terms of corporate financial reporting, Enron originally engaged in fairly straightforward accounting practices. In each reporting time period, the company produced a balance sheet that revealed the costs involved in distributing its energy products, and the revenues they generated by selling those products. However, as Enron grew over time, the company's business model itself became so complex that for many, it ended up being incomprehensible. Thus, keeping accurate accounting records became extremely difficult, while presenting a false image of the company's financial picture became easier. "The

Enron scandal grew out of a steady accumulation of habits and values and actions that began years before, and finally spiraled out of control," authors Bethany McLean and Peter Elkind conclude.[6]

Among those troublesome "habits and values and actions" were some very questionable accounting practices. For one, Enron relied heavily upon management forecasts as a basis for present-day assessments of the company's performance. Enron also engaged in the creation of "Special Purpose Entities," which were, in effect, separate corporations that enabled Enron to off-load some of their debt and expenses so as to make Enron's official accounting books appear better. These tactics, among others, created a very skewed picture of Enron's actual performance and provided a way for the management team to line their pockets with an ever-rising stock price.

These tactics . . . provided a way for the management team to line their pockets with an ever-rising stock price.

Perhaps most telling about Enron's faulty accounting is the behavior of the company's own audit committee. At the time of Enron's downfall, a corporation's audit committee typically was comprised of people with only limited backgrounds in accounting or finance. Enron's audit committee, however, consisted of people with more expertise than most. Yet despite this higher than usual level of expertise, Enron's audit committee still did not have the insight to adequately question the company and its auditors. Worse still, the audit committee was reported to have been pressured by company management to not ask probing questions.

As for Arthur Andersen's role in the scandal, their questionable conduct seems to have fallen into two broad categories. For one, Arthur Andersen not only provided auditing services to Enron, but they also provided business consultancy services. This established a clear conflict-of-interest scenario between the two companies. In fact, in the year 2000, the Arthur Andersen corporation earned $25 million from Enron for providing auditing services, yet earned even more—another $27 million—for consulting to Enron. For Arthur Andersen to have called "foul" on Enron's internal accounting practices would have been to call "foul" with one of its own, lucrative consulting clients. This dual role that Arthur Andersen played in the Enron Corporation was later addressed in the law resulting from Enron's downfall.

Another area of misconduct within the Arthur Andersen company involved a much more intentional act. In 2002, company officials were convicted of "obstruction of justice," for having actively shredded documents pertinent to the auditing of Enron. Two managers, in particular, were identified as having given orders to destroy documents, in an attempt to protect Enron.

People from within both the Enron and Arthur Andersen organizations behaved very badly. Their bad behavior led to the destruction of lives and careers and reputations, the loss of opportunity for hundreds of thousands, and the loss of investment and retirement funds for investors. Yet, it wasn't just the "cheaters" who got hurt. The majority of the employees in these respective organizations did not behave badly, and yet everyone involved experienced the pain.

Was greed involved in the downfall of these companies? It's difficult to imagine that it was not. Managers eager to add some "fast money" were willing to violate law and jeopardize two large organizations for their own selfish pursuits.

THE UNWISE LAW THAT FOLLOWED

But the damage didn't end with twenty-three convictions and the loss of two companies, three lives, $11 billion in wealth, and 100,000 jobs. The ultimate response to the crisis from both the United States Congress and the president was also damaging. The law that resulted from the aftermath of the scandal brought about a loss of freedom within our free-market capitalistic economic system.

As one might expect, U.S. lawmakers reacted with outrage when Enron declared bankruptcy, as details began to emerge about the internal behavior at both the Enron Corporation and Arthur Andersen. During the congressional investigations that followed, Congressman James Greenwood summed up the sentiment on Capitol Hill fairly succinctly: "Enron robbed the bank [and] Arthur Andersen provided the getaway car."[7]

In the face of the story that was emerging, outrage and disgust were warranted. But misbehavior by participants in our free-market economic system, especially highly paid participants who control a lot of other people's money,

127

also affirms the worst stereotypes of capitalism, and it gives elected public-policy makers opportunity to try and save the day by constructing policies that constrain the free-market system.

This is precisely what happened after the Enron scandal, as the U.S. Congress and President George W. Bush soon passed into law what has become known as the Sarbanes-Oxley Act.

Officially named the Public Company Accounting Reform and Investor Protection Act of 2002, the bill was sponsored by Senator Paul Sarbanes (D-Maryland) and Representative Michael Oxley (R-Ohio). In light of the magnitude of the scandal, Congress was eager to do *something* about it, and to act quickly. And in response to the Enron scandal, as it was unfolding in 2002, Oxley managed to get a version of the bill passed in the House of Representatives on April 25 of that year, Sarbanes got a Senate version passed on July 15, and by July 24, Congress approved the official Sarbanes-Oxley Act of 2002 with an overwhelming 423–9 victory in the House, and a margin of 99–0 in the Senate. When he signed the bill into law a week later, President Bush described it as providing "the most far-reaching reforms of American business practices since the time of [President] Franklin D. Roosevelt."

The Sarbanes-Oxley Act . . . ultimately renders our free-market economy less free and less productive.

With congressional vote margins like these, it's probably safe to say that at the time of its passage, the law was popular and well-received by the American people. And as you're reading this now, you may be more convinced than ever that, in light of the horrible behavior at Enron and Arthur Andersen, a swift crackdown by Congress was warranted, and that the U.S. government needed to step in and prevent another Enron from ever happening again.

We have reiterated throughout this book our position on appropriate regulation of free-market enterprise; capitalism is not "unfettered" (it certainly is not in the United States), nor should it be. Yet we also believe that the Sarbanes-Oxley Act is an example of a heavy-handed law that punishes even the business people who behave appropriately, and ultimately renders our free-market economy less free, and less productive.

In many ways, the Sarbanes-Oxley Act (which is often abbreviated as Sarbox) provides a mirror image to the Enron scandal, and addresses the failings of Enron in a point-for-point fashion. One of the main components of the law is the mandated establishment of the Public Company Accounting Oversight Board, a private-sector, nonprofit corporation that oversees all auditors of publicly traded corporations. The board of the PCAOB consists of five members, all of whom are appointed by the SEC, and while it is a private sector entity, it does nonetheless fulfill many governmental-type regulatory functions. These relatively new regulatory functions are funded with an annual budget of approximately $100 million, money that is collected in fees charged to the issuers of securities.

Now, consider the implications of what we're describing here. Powerful professionals at a handful of corporations cheat; the companies are destroyed; Congress takes action to "correct" the problem; and the result is, among other things, the creation of a new regulatory bureaucracy that takes approximately $100 million away from participants in the securities market. You may believe that this is fair, or reasonable, or necessary "regulation." There is no disputing that this results in less freedom in the economy—investors and securities firms have approximately $100 million of their money taken away from them each year as a result of the scandal. Some people cheat, and as a result, everybody, even people who play by the rules, pay the price.

Another section of the Sarbox law imposed new federal requirements on accounting firms that perform auditing services. As a result, accounting firms have to file additional, more frequent auditing reports and to comply with strict federal standards to ensure that they are not creating a conflict of interest by providing both auditing and other services, such as consulting, to the same client simultaneously (another direct response to the Arthur Andersen role in the Enron scandal). Again, you may say that's appropriate regulation.[8] But here again, it leaves accountants and auditors with less freedom in the marketplace, while more time and energy and resources are spent demonstrating that they are in compliance with the law.

Other portions of the law require publicly traded companies to demonstrate that their senior executives are taking personal responsibility for the completeness and accuracy of their corporate financial reports, and impose enhanced reporting requirements for financial transactions within companies. The resources that publicly traded companies now must spend to comply with federal law are resources taken away from the development of new products and services, and from a company's employees and investors. One scandal, and one law, has resulted in less freedom and less productivity.

We are certainly not alone in our conclusion that Sarbox had harmful unintended consequences. Indeed, there is broad consensus on this issue. For example, economic commentator Steve Forbes, while agreeing reforms of our financial system are essential, describes Sarbox as being both "costly" and "punitive."[9] And in January 2007, then–House Minority Leader Nancy Pelosi (D-California) noted that Sarbox was so overreaching that it had brought about "unintended consequences."[10]

"GETTING EVEN" WITH CULPRITS
(BOTH PERCEIVED AND REAL)

The Sarbanes-Oxley Act is but one example of law that was crafted specifically to address a wrongdoing in the economy. It is not the only example of public policy that is intended to help but ends up hurting. Recall from our discussions in chapters 5 and 6 how the U.S. Congress and two different presidents sought to proactively help in the subprime mortgage crisis yet ended up doing some very harmful and destructive things in the process.

We recognize that participants in our capitalistic economic system can at times be motivated by greed and will at times make bad choices. We also recognize that this dilemma doesn't just apply to business executives or accountants. Those in public office have an obvious need to curry the favor of voters, and sometimes they will say and do whatever is necessary to keep voters happy, whether or not their actions and proposals are productive.

We are not making a "political statement" here, nor are we making a statement about any particular political ideology or party. The Sarbox bill was crafted by members of both the Republican and Democratic political parties, and it passed overwhelmingly in both chambers of the legislature. Thus our critique of this bill is a critique that applies equally to both sides of the political aisle. More importantly, our critique is a statement about the imperfection of human nature, and how those imperfections can impact the behavior of public policy makers, as well as business people.

Of further concern to us are laws passed not to delimit greed but to appease envy. Trying to appease people's frustration can result in harmful public policy. Here are just three examples of poor public policy decisions.

The Windfall Profits Tax. For several months during the 2008 U.S. presidential election campaign, the world endured a sharp rise in global oil prices. This resulted in a steady and dramatic increase in, among other things, gasoline prices in the United States. From the campaign trail, then-Senator Barack Obama, as many other presidents and presidential candidates had done previously, proposed a new tax on the so-called windfall profits that American oil companies were allegedly reaping, while the American consumer was allegedly being victimized by the oil companies' greed.

"I'll make oil companies like Exxon pay a tax on their windfall profits," candidate Obama stated in June of that year, "and we'll use the money to help families pay for their skyrocketing energy costs and other bills." It made for great campaign rhetoric, and the idea was well received. But would it have made sense economically? Would it have improved conditions for American consumers, and lowered the price of gasoline?

By October, petroleum prices had begun to fall again, and candidate discussions on how to lower the prices had been all but forgotten. But as a policy idea, the proposal was destructive on multiple fronts. For one, the price of oil on the global market is such a complex matter that American oil companies, alone, can't control

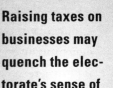

Raising taxes on businesses may quench the electorate's sense of envy, but consumers themselves end up paying the penalty.

them entirely. Significantly, the profit margin of American oil companies remained relatively steady even during the "price spike," in part because the oil industry is a global enterprise.

Secondly, the U.S. government already taxes American companies, oil companies and non-oil companies alike. The notion that the government would levy an additional tax on "windfall profits" (that is, profits that are "too high") in one particular industry, and the result would be a "better deal" for consumers of that industry, is foolishness. The fact is that, ultimately, corporations themselves don't pay their taxes. The costs that companies bear in taxes are factored in to the prices of their products and services, and, thus, individual consumers ultimately pay those taxes. Raising taxes on businesses may quench the electorate's sense of envy and need for vengeance, but consumers themselves end up paying the penalty.

Minimum Wage Laws. Using the power of government to mandate the minimum wage that employers can pay their workers is a popular idea with many voters, and the practice has been around for many years. Historically, minimum wage laws were originally utilized in the United States to help remedy the abuses of so-called "sweatshops" where workers—often women and children—labored in dangerous conditions for long stretches of time and for unjustly low wages.

Yet today, while concerns about working environments and child labor have long since been addressed by other regulatory policies, minimum wage laws still exist. And among advocates of minimum wage laws, rarely is the perspective of the business owner considered.

From the vantage point of a business owner, a government mandate to pay a higher minimum wage quite easily translates into a smaller budget with which to pay employees and can lead to fewer people being hired. Thus there is great agreement among economists about the negative effect that minimum wage laws have upon the rate of employment.

But the prospect of less employment hasn't lessened the popularity of minimum wage laws. Indeed, the federal government mandated a minimum wage increase in July 2009—in the midst of the Great Recession—at a time when the national unemployment rate had already risen to 9.5 percent, discouraging hiring even further.[11]

Executive Compensation Limits. The idea of limiting the amount of income that corporate executives are permitted to earn is a popular idea among many Americans today. And as we pointed out in chapter 6, President Obama's administration is moving forward on efforts to limit executive compensation (the efforts are being mandated for companies that received government "bailout" money), as President Obama has appointed an "executive compensation czar" (the technical title is "special master for compensation").

The effort to regulate executive pay may be motivated, in part, by a lack of respect for the free market and a preference for a more government-controlled economic system. But political motives may also be spurring the drive to limit executive compensation. Politicians have much to gain by influencing the free-market economy in ways that appeal to voters' sense of envy. Curtailing the income of so-called rich, greedy executives is a way to make this kind of appeal. Yet as we noted earlier, limiting the income of executives doesn't provide those executives the incentive to perform more responsibly and to produce better results. Indeed, there are ways to incentivize these kinds of improvements, but placing a governmental "cap" on their income is not one of them.[12]

Without a doubt, in the capitalistic economic system people sometimes choose to act badly. And as we have seen, bad behavior can produce devastating consequences. Yet we can also be assured that politicians can be equally as selfish, as they seek to gain the favor of their constituents by enacting market "reforms" and protections. In order for American capitalism to achieve its ideals and possibilities going forward, the American electorate will need to become more discerning as to the differences between greed and envy, and between economic policies that help and those that hurt.

NOTES

1. Charles Hurt, "Obama Fires a 'Robin Hood' Warning Shot," *New York Post*, 15 October 2008. Obama was speaking to Joe Wurzelbacher—who went on to become known as "Joe the Plumber" during the 2008 presidential campaign.

2. Shawn Tully, "Meet the 23,000% Stock," *Fortune*, 14 September 2003.

3. David Ellis, "Countrywide Rescue: $4 Billion," CNN Money, January 11, 2008, http://money.cnn.com/2008/01/11/news/companies/boa_countrywide/index.htm?cnn=yes.

4. Reported at www.ag.ca.gov/newsalerts/release.php?id=1618.

5. See Rand's classic work on this, *The Virtue of Selfishness* (New York: Signet, 1964).

6. Bethany McLean and Peter Elkind, *The Smartest Guys in the Room: The Amazing Rise and Scandalous Fall of Enron* (New York: Penguin, 2003). See also the film by the same title. For further reading on Enron's demise, see Nancy Rapoport and Bala G. Dharan, eds., *Enron: Corporate Fiascos and Their Implications* (New York: Foundation Press, 2003), and Kurt Eichenwald, *Conspiracy of Fools* (New York: Broadway Books, 2005).

7. Kwame Holman, "Investigating Enron," *Online NewsHour*, 24 January 2002, http://www.pbs.org/newshour/bb/business/jan-june02/enron_1-24.html.

8. We think this may have been a good thing that eliminates a clear conflict of interest between auditing and consulting. The counterargument to that is that who better to provide consulting services to a company than one who knows its books so well? One obvious conflict occurs when an auditor designs and implements a company's financial controls system—and then audits the effectiveness of its own system.

9. Steve Forbes, "How Capitalism Will Save Us," *Forbes*, 10 November 2008, at http://www.forbes.com/forbes/2008/1110/018.html.

10. John Berlau, "Democrats: There Is Such a Thing as Too Much Regulation," Business and Media Institute, 3 January 2007, at http://www.businessandmedia.org/commentary/2007/20070103153849.aspx.

11. Declan McCullagh, "Minimum Wage Hike Could Lead to Job Losses," *CBS News*, 21 July 2009, http://www.cbsnews.com/ blogs/2009/07/21/business/econwatch/entry5178888.shtml. As noted in chapter 5, many national leaders have termed the massive economic downturn of 2008-2009 the worst recession of the past eighty years; hence the term the *Great Recession*.

12. John Tamny, "Banker Pay Curbs Won't Work," *Orange County Register*, 25 September 2009, http://www.ocregister.com/opinion/pay-firms-financial-2581597-work-street.

Capitalism is surely the worst economic system,
except for all the others that have been tried.

—WINSTON CHURCHILL

8

CAPITALISM CAN'T DO IT ALL

You've probably realized by now: We think capitalism is good.

We are advocates of what capitalism has done, and what it can do, to lift living standards around the world. We believe that economic matters are moral issues that deserve our attention and passion in the same way that other moral issues, such as abortion, physician-assisted suicide, and capital punishment, capture our focus.

We have argued that the free-market system is consistent with the Bible, while at the same time not insisting that it was "handed down from on high." We further argued that capitalism both needs, and nurtures, some of the most important virtues that, as a society, we hold dear. And we are also aware of some of the major criticisms of the free market and believe that most of them have satisfactory answers, though we acknowledge that some of the criticisms do have merit.

We have insisted that the current economic downturn is not a failure of capitalism, but a failure of the financial system. What went wrong is that the combination of government incentives and shortsighted policy (including some of the deregulation of the financial system) created conditions in which corporate and individual greed flourished. And moving into the future, we believe that, generally speaking, the more that economic freedom can be unleashed, the better it is for generating prosperity.

But we also acknowledge that the market has limits, that forms of regulation are necessary, and that a variety of institutions need to contribute to setting limits on the pursuit of self-interest. You may think that this is somewhat obvious, given the economic crisis of the early 2000s, and we would tend to agree. Limits on the market have always been the norm, not the exception.

The *pure* free market has never existed in real life—only in the world of economic theory. This is especially true in the banking sector that has suffered such a collapse in the late 2000s. That sector has always been heavily regulated, though some of the deregulation of financial markets that occurred earlier in the 2000s looks from our current vantage point to have been unwise.

We will suggest that regulation and capitalism are not fundamentally inconsistent. Capitalism has always had regulation and Adam Smith himself did not envision a market without any external restraints. We will further argue that there are some goods and services that ought not be on the market.

Thus the limits of the free market are the subject of this final chapter. We want to suggest that the economic system is a part of the whole society—an important part, to be sure (recall that we began this book by noting that economics affects every area of a person's life). Yet it also must be balanced by other important segments of society. We are not libertarians who would insist that there is little, if any, place for government in economic life and that the market is best left completely on its own.

ASSUMPTIONS ABOUT THE MARKET

From the start, we are assuming that *the market is not entirely self-correcting;* that is, the market *by itself* is not capable of always providing its own checks and balances. It is true that one of the compelling features of capitalism is its ability to adjust to changing conditions and shift the allocation of resources efficiently. But the market needs other components of society to provide these checks and balances.

Even if the market were entirely self-correcting, we would still insist that there's a legitimate place for other institutions that balance the market. This is because there's always a time lag involved in market corrections, when people invariably get hurt. For example, it takes time for information about harmful products to become widespread enough for consumers to stop buying the products. And during that time, consumers are at risk of being harmed by these products.

We are further assuming that the family, voluntary associations, and religious groups and other mediating institutions stand between the individual and the state, with an important role to play in setting limits on the pursuit of economic self-interest. These institutions often affirm the virtues necessary for the market to function properly. We take it as practically self-evident that some forms of government regulation are appropriate and necessary to ensure just and fair transactions, prevent fraud, and keep consumers safe. This must be done carefully in order to prevent both the overreaching of the law and the all-too-common unintended consequences of government's excessive involvement in economic affairs.

WHAT MAKES A MARKET SYSTEM THRIVE?

Believe it or not, we actually don't believe that the free market is for everyone. The reason for this is that there are *places that are not well suited for the introduction of market capitalism.* For example, it is widely held that capitalism was initiated prematurely in the former Soviet Union in the early 1990s. The conditions necessary for capitalism to exist and to thrive were not present at that time, and this resulted in a corrupt version of capitalism becoming the dominant economic force. Additionally, there are some countries/cultures in sub-Saharan Africa that lack the necessary social structures, such as widespread legal recognition of private property, that make it very difficult for free market institutions to gain a foothold.

Certain conditions and social structures must be present in a society in order for capitalism to flourish, as well as some virtues for capitalism to function as it was intended (see chapter 3). Those conditions and virtues are good for everyone, and cultures that function according to them are more likely to experience prosperity. But to introduce free-market capitalism without those critical pre-conditions is somewhat like planting a seed in hostile ground where it cannot grow.

So let's think further about the conditions necessary for the market system to flourish. When Adam Smith conceived of capitalism, he did not advocate a system in which self-interest was the only motivation that mattered for the proper function of the market. He did *not* suggest, as the popular interpretation of Smith by the economist George Stigler maintained, that "*The Wealth of Nations* is a stupendous palace erected upon the granite of self-interest."[1]

Smith argued instead that a critical ingredient for the market to flourish was for individuals to restrain their self-interest. He urged this by invoking other balancing virtues, such as benevolence, thrift, prudence, justice, and cooperation. This was not only because restraining one's self-interest in the short term benefited the person for the long term, but also because, according to Smith, these balancing virtues are consistent with our better nature.

> **Smith argued the market could not function without other balancing virtues of benevolence . . . justice, and cooperation.**

These virtues emerge out of the "social passions" which Smith outlined in depth in *The Theory of Moral Sentiments*. He advocated an *enlightened self-interest*, in which the pursuit of one's interests is checked by other aspects of human nature, and thus contribute to the market functioning in a fair and just manner.[2] In fact, according to Smith, the market could not function justly without these balancing virtues. He did not assume that human beings would always or even consistently act in this way, but he acknowledged that the work of the "invisible hand," in which the individual pursuits of self-interest resulted in the common good, was dependent on self-interest being balanced by a concern for justice and cooperation.

In short, the "providential" aspect of the invisible hand of the market produced an aggregate benefit to society as a whole, only as long as self-interest was tempered by other virtues. He would surely have condemned the excesses of greed as inconsistent not only with a properly functioning competitive market, but also with human nature.[3]

CHECKS AND BALANCES FOR THE ECONOMIC SYSTEM

For capitalism to function as it was intended, individual self-interest must be balanced by the virtues undergirding restraint. Yet, on a broader scale, the economic system must be checked by other social institutions as well. These institutions must create the proper context in which the economic system operates. They consist of the formal political system—our structure of government policies and regulations that we have discussed throughout this book —and what theologian Michael Novak calls the more informal "moral-cultural system," which includes such voluntary associations as religious organizations, schools, the family, and other charitable organizations.[4]

Both provide essential restraints on the potential excesses of the economic system. Each offers incentives and reinforcement for the kind of virtuous behavior that is necessary for market mechanisms to function as they are designed. This is not a particularly new idea, since capitalism has always been regulated to some degree, and since the many institutions of the moral-cultural system have long spoken to matters of economic life. Yet it is an important idea that needs to be reiterated. The political system provides the necessary legal structure in which the market system operates. That is, without a functional government that can provide stability and structure, a society will not be well suited for capitalism, and it may be unwise to introduce it into such a society. But not just any political system will suffice. Particular elements must be in place within the political system in order for the market system to flourish.

For example, *the rule of law* must be widely respected in any culture in which capitalism is expected to succeed. In the absence of the rule of law, a society will end up with black markets, mob capitalism, or crony capitalism, all undesirable forms of a distorted market system. The rule of law must be in place so that political stability is ensured—so that companies, investors, and entrepreneurs will be confident that their long-term investments in doing business in that region will pay off. In countries where the rule of law is not well established, there is no such certainty, and, not surprisingly, those areas generally have great difficulty attracting outside investment. More specifically, respect for the rule of law must involve a legal system that enforces contracts, prosecutes fraud, and protects fairness in business dealings.

In addition, the political system must provide *protection for private property*. Private ownership of property is vital to the proper functioning of capitalism (see chapter 6). A society's political system must safeguard the rights to private property in order for capitalism to succeed. Recognized rights of ownership that provide protection from arbitrary seizure are critical in order to encourage the necessary risk taking by investors. Without property rights, it is difficult to see how social mobility is possible, since there is no foundation for the accumulation of wealth.

If a businessperson is not sure that he/she will be able to maintain ownership of their property (including both their investment capital and their profit) in a particular country or region, there is a strong disincentive to conducting business in such a region. Companies that are at risk of having their operations nationalized or otherwise seized are likewise understandably hesitant to invest in operations in those regions where property rights are not enforced. Vigorously enforced property rights are thus essential for a productive economy, since the prospect of accumulating property and bettering one's financial condition are critical incentives that encourage initiative and risk taking.

There are other legal protections that must be in place in order to provide incentives for enterprise and entrepreneurial activity. For example, the political system must provide something like *patent laws* and protection for intellectual property to safeguard inventiveness and risk taking. Laws protecting patents reward creativity, imagination, and resourcefulness. Imagine a system in which the design for a new product, service, or technology could be pirated easily by another individual or company. This would seriously discourage entrepreneurs from taking the risks necessary for bringing new innovations to the market.

As important as a stable political system based on the rule of law is for capitalism, the moral-cultural system plays a critical role as well. Novak insists that "the moral-cultural system is the chief dynamic force behind the rise both of a democratic political system and of a liberal (in the classical sense with its emphasis on individual freedom and limited government) economic system.

The moral cultural system is the *sine qua non* of the political system and the economic system."[5] It reinforces the incentives provided by the political system, as it provides a moral foundation for personal habits and behaviors necessary for prosperity.

The moral-cultural system, influenced by religious and voluntary organizations, serves as a mediating structure that validates and reinforces restraints on the pursuit of self-interest. It does this by nurturing the values and virtues we discussed in chapter 3 and by reminding the culture in various ways that life is not reducible to economics. Those values and incentives support the notion that human beings are more than economic actors and the goals of life are more than the accumulation of wealth. They also strengthen the bonds of trust and community, trust being a critical component of an environment conducive to economic growth.[6]

Both Adam Smith and the American founders envisioned an economic system checked by the political system and the mediating structures of the culture. They insisted that the market needs supervision, both from the formal government and from the informal institutions that have traditionally been the guardians of values and virtues. There is clearly a place for regulation and for government to intervene in the market to protect consumers and ensure fair dealings. And the moral cultural system must provide moral parameters for the economic system, reinforcing government's role.

GOODS/SERVICES THAT ARE "OFF THE MARKET"

We agree with capitalism's critics that some goods and services just shouldn't be bought or sold. Of course, there is considerable debate about what those nonmarket goods and services ought to be. But the fact that there is debate on this is an indication of a rough consensus that the market should not distribute *everything*.

One example on which virtually everyone agrees today is that *human beings* should not be bought and sold. Although more people are in slavery internationally than ever before, human trafficking is nearly universally condemned as immoral.

One of the main reasons that slavery was first abolished in the West is because human beings were seen to possess fundamental dignity by virtue of being made in God's image. Being treated as an object for purchase and sale on the open market came to be considered a violation of this intrinsic dignity that every person has. The Thirteenth Amendment to the U.S. Constitution abolished slavery because it was considered intrinsically immoral to own another person, regardless of how that person was treated. In fact, from the perspective of the Thirteenth Amendment, the ways in which slaves were treated was irrelevant—it was the very fact that they were slaves at all that was objectionable.

So at first glance, there's not much debate about buying and selling human beings. But there may be more than you think. Take, for example, the idea that *adoptable children* should be distributed according to free-market dynamics. That's an idea that's been seriously proposed, on the grounds that it would be a far more efficient way to administer adoptions.[7] It might also provide an incentive for financially and emotionally overwhelmed unwed mothers to put their children up for adoption, into homes in which they could be properly raised and cared for. Of course, the counterarguments to this, which most people find compelling, are that it could lead to unwed mothers being exploited (due to financial needs) and that it would lead to the best interests of the child being minimized or ignored outright. Bringing money into the situation could bring about an element of coercion to the woman, with her dire financial situation the reason why she is considering something she would otherwise never consider. Her vulnerability, which comes as a result of her unwanted pregnancy and inability to provide for her child, makes her an easy mark for manipulation and exploitation by those who would prey on her.

If adoption becomes a financial transaction in the open market, another potential problem would be no assurance that the baby would go to parents who are fit for the task of parenting. The only thing that matters is their ability to pay for adoption itself, not their ability to parent. It further creates the risk that babies will be stolen from families in order to sell profitably on the open market. In fact, there is already a sizeable black market for stolen children all over the world—and that's with black market adoptions being illegal in most places.

Regardless of how you weigh these arguments, there is still a considerable consensus, and in our view, rightly so, that children should not be objects for purchase and sale on the open market.[8] That's a limit on the market that is widely accepted.

TO MARKET, TO MARKET:
HUMAN ORGANS, PROSTITUTION, ILLEGAL DRUGS?

Another example is more controversial. That's the view that *transplantable organs* should be available for purchase and sale on the open market, especially organs that can be harvested from living donors, such as kidneys. The argument is that providing a financial incentive would increase the much-needed supply of organs for transplant, and might motivate more people to designate themselves as donors upon their death. But selling organs has long been illegal in much of the world, for reasons similar to the previous prohibition on adoption for sale: the widespread concern that financial distress would compel someone to do something that he or she would never consider, were it not for their severe financial difficulty.

For example, very few people would consider giving up one of their kidneys, except for a child or close relative (in which case, money is not normally a factor). Fewer still would consider it under normal circumstances, because, even though you need only one kidney, most people consider it a wise backup plan to keep their other one. But if there's serious financial misfortune, the money could put that option on the table for alleviating their financial problems. It could function in a coercive way to force someone to make a decision that they would never otherwise consider.

In addition, organs are still donated, not sold, today because if there were a market for organs, the rich would always be able to bid up the price to be out of reach of the less fortunate. The poor would rarely, if ever, receive organ transplants, since the available supply would be purchased by the well-off who could afford them. We rightly distribute organs on a combined acute-need, first-come, first-served basis, so that the ability to pay, one's "social worth," or other merit-based grounds can't be used as the basis for distributing scarce organs. This helps ensure that the poor have as much right to essential organs for transplants as the wealthy.[9]

There is further concern that if everything is reduced to market transactions, there would be no room left for altruism. If heroic acts of organ donation were to become mere market transactions, then the place of selfless giving is reduced and possibly forced out of the public currency altogether.[10] In our view, transplantable organs are what are called "market inalienable," that is, not subject to market transactions because of the prospect of coercion, exploitation, and the undermining of altruism.

Some debate exists over other goods and services. For example, sexual services have long been considered off the market because of the harm, both physically and morally, that is associated with prostitution. There is also concern about the prospect for exploitation of vulnerable women and children who are forced into prostitution because of financial hardship. Some feminists have argued that it's a woman's choice to do with her body as she chooses, including sell it for sex. Other debated goods and services include the sale of eggs and sperm and the rental of wombs, otherwise known as surrogate motherhood. Again there is concern about women being coerced and exploited to do things that they would not otherwise ever consider on their merits—they are only being driven by financial distress.

Further, there is some discussion of whether some illegal drugs, especially marijuana, should be sold on the open market via the decriminalizing of drugs. The argument is that the war on drugs is a costly failure, and keeping drugs illegal has driven up the costs and the crime involved with the drug trade. The counterargument is that something as harmful as street drugs have no business being on the open market at all.

Resolving these debates is beyond the scope of this book. What these discussions illustrate, however, is that there is a consensus that some things do not belong as market transactions. Most of the debate over the specific goods and services is over the merits of making those things available on the market. Hardly anyone suggests that everything should be available on the market.

SHOULD HEALTH CARE REMAIN A MARKET TRANSACTION?

A major recent point of debate in this area is whether or not *health care* should continue to be a market transaction. Proponents of a single-payer (that is, fully government run and financed) health-care system insist that health care is a right that should be provided irrespective of someone's ability to pay for it. Their view is that health care, since it is so fundamental to a person's survival and well-being, ought not be distributed according to market mechanisms of supply, demand, and price. On the other hand, those who favor more of a market approach to health care argue that there is nothing wrong with health care being allocated by means of the market, since health care is fundamentally a commodity similar to other commodities that are critical for a person's well-being.

When someone insists that health care is a right, we must first clarify exactly what is meant by that claim. And to arrive at this understanding, it's important to realize that philosophers distinguish between *positive* and *negative rights*. Negative rights are personal rights to be left alone to pursue one's goals and ambitions apart from government, or anyone else's, intrusion. They are a person's rights of noninterference. Many of the rights outlined in the Constitution are considered negative rights, such as freedom of religion, free speech, and the right of peaceable assembly.

But some others, such as the right to a fair trial by a jury of one's peers, are understood to be positive rights. A positive right requires someone else to provide the right in question, and if a cost is involved, to pay for it. The right to a fair trial is something that must be provided by government in order for citizens to exercise their right to due process of law. Many rights that are invoked today, such as the right to an education, are considered positive rights. And proponents of a right to health care conceive of that right as a positive right too, obligating the community to provide for it.

Health care is widely viewed as a positive right today. But a government-run, single-payer system for all of health care does not necessarily follow from the notion that it is a positive right.

We would suggest that the health-care market is somewhat skewed, since the vast majority of health care is paid for by third-party payers, such as insurance companies, and the insurance premiums are often not paid by individuals but by their employers. Anytime someone else is paying for something, the tendency is to overconsume that product or service, making it very difficult to keep costs down, which is one reason (though not the only one) why the costs of health care continue to rise. In our view, "unskewing" the market would make a good deal of sense, so that the market could function properly and competition could help keep prices under control. This would involve, minimally, using insurance for catastrophes, in the same way we use auto insurance (we don't expect our auto insurance to pay for our oil changes and gas!), allowing for insurance companies to compete nationally and expanding the tax advantages and incentives for medical savings accounts (at the least, allowing them to roll over from year to year).

To be clear, we view health care as more of a commodity than a right. It's not that different from food and housing—both essential to well-being and flourishing. But we don't have a single payer for either and few people think that's something worth considering. We have a vigorous market for both food and housing, and those who cannot afford them are given help, through food stamps, subsidized housing, and various private-sector charity efforts. Government supplements the market.

> **Market competition is the best option for holding down medical costs.**

We consider government assistance for health care to be similar—it supplements the market and provides for the less fortunate without it being necessary to involve a comprehensive, single-payer government provider.

We do recognize that there is one important difference between health care and food/housing. Sometimes health care has an urgency to it that makes it difficult to "shop around" for the lowest price and best service. This is why we suggest that insurance function for those emergency situations, but that for other non-urgent and preventive care, people should have, and sometimes do have, the ability to allow for market competition to work. For example, the LASIK eye surgery that corrects nearsightedness is a nonemergency procedure that has seen its price come down dramatically over the years, primarily due to competition among the service providers. The same is true of many cosmetic surgical procedures. The notion of "direct primary care" where patients directly pay clinics for routine doctor visits is another place where competition can help lower prices.[11] We don't see any good reason to see health care as one of those services that ought to be off the market. In fact, we see market competition as the best option for holding the costs of care down.

THE BEST HOPE FOR THE POOR

Though we are certainly proponents of more free markets as the way to prosperity, we acknowledge that capitalism functions within important limits set by both government and the mediating institutions of the culture. It has always been that way, from its ideological roots in Adam Smith to the present day. We have attempted to offer a case for capitalism within those limits as consistent with the Bible and some very important social virtues. Indeed, capitalism both requires and nurtures those virtues.

The criticisms of capitalism are not new, and we have tried to explain what happened with the recent Great Recession. We suggested that more free markets are generally better for prosperity, while at the same time acknowledging that some market regulation is necessary and appropriate—and that capitalism has always been somewhat regulated.

Since the inception of industrial capitalism, more than half of the world's population has been lifted out of grinding poverty. To be sure, the other half is critically important, and in our view, the expansion of capitalism and free markets is a vital part of the solution. Of course, certain political and social conditions are necessary for the market to flourish, but if they are in place, we insist that capitalism is indeed the best hope for the poor around the world.

NOTES

1. George Stigler, "Smith's Travels on the Ship of State," *History of Political Economy*, 3 (1971): 265.

2. Patricia H. Werhane, *Adam Smith and His Legacy for Modern Capitalism* (New York: Oxford Univ. Press, 1991), 108–109.

3. Ibid., 88.

4. The discussion of the three realms of society is taken from Michael Novak, *The Spirit of Democratic Capitalism* (New York: Simon and Schuster, 1982), 171–86. Our discussion is in contrast to that of sociologist Daniel Bell, who saw these three areas in conflict, producing the contradictions of society. See Daniel Bell, *The Cultural Contradictions of Capitalism* (New York: Basic Books, 1976), 10.

5. Novak, *The Spirit of Democratic Capitalism*, 185.

6. See Francis Fukuyama, *Trust: The Social Virtues and the Creation of Prosperity* (New York: Free Press, 1995).

7. This was proposed by appeals court judge Richard Posner in the widely read article by E. M. Landes and R. A. Posner, "The Economics of the Baby Shortage." *Journal of Legal Studies 7* (June 1978): 323–48. See also R. A. Posner, "The Regulation of the Market in Adoptions." *Boston University Law Review 67* (January 1987): 59–72. For a more moderate view, see Donald J. Boudreaux, " A Modest Proposal to Regulate Infant Adoptions," *Cato Journal* 15: 1 (1995), www.cato.org/pubs.

8. In our view, some forms of surrogate motherhood amount to baby-selling too. When the surrogate contributes the egg and womb both, she is the mother of the child, under most definitions. When she gives up her maternal rights to her child and hands over the child, all in exchange for a fee (that exceeds her expenses), that constitutes baby-selling and should be illegal (and in many states, it is). See Scott B. Rae, *The Ethics of Commercial Surrogate Motherhood* (Westport, Conn.: Praeger, 1994).

9. For more on this, see Margaret J. Radin, *Contested Commodities: The Trouble with Trade in Sex, Children, Body Parts and Other Things* (Cambridge, Mass.: Harvard Univ. Press, 1996).

10. See Richard A. Titmuss, *The Gift Relationship: From Human Blood to Social Policy* (New York: New Press, 1997).

11. Clark S. Judge, "Wednesday's Speech Won't Hit Reset Button for Obamacare," White House Writers Group, 7 September 2009, http://www.whwg.com/thefirm/sample.php/265/Clark_S._Judge.

ACKNOWLEDGMENTS

It is an honor and a pleasure to have collaborated with my coauthor, Dr. Scott Rae, on this project. May the world enjoy a brighter future because of our efforts!

A big thank-you to my friends at Northfield Publishing, especially Madison Trammel and Jim Vincent. Your professionalism and ability to capture the vision of this project have made all the difference.

My thanks also to Richard Bhella, a "true Brit" and dedicated historian who offered valuable advice as I was summarizing the history of precapitalist England in chapter 3.

I am also grateful to Hugh Hallman, my friend, my attorney, and in every sense a true statesman, and his wife, Dr. Susan Hallman. Thanks also to my friend and mentor Bob Shank and his wife, Cheri Shank; to Matt and Kim McMahon; Brad and Julie Hahn; Tony and Bobbie Valente; Fred and Sally Baker; Clark and Margo Judge; and Paul and Diane Patterson. Your lives, your diligent work, and your generosity exemplify the virtues of capitalism and the best that our free-market economic system has to offer. Thank you for your examples.

My gratitude to the many friends who have helped to shape my view of the world over the years: Chris Bassett, Steve and Ja Betts, Chuck and Pam Booher, Chris Bowen, Diane Bower, Mike Churchin, Rev. Charley Coppinger, Bob Donaldson, Dr. Bill Dyment, Lt. Col. Rick Erickson, Dee Dee Fleming, Kent Forde, Stan Hill, Cal Jernigan, John and Betsy Kaiser, Laura and Bob Knaperek, Mark and Melodie Leon, Kris Mauren, Todd Minturn, Dr. Steve Morgan, Cheryl Nation, Vernon Parker, Kevin and Laura Rice, Dr. Pamela Ann Rice, Onnie and Brian Shekerjian, Father Robert Sirico, David Smith, Dr. Dave Stoop, Jon Talbert, Dr. John Townsend, Barbara X. White, and Tony Yim.

Finally, a big thank-you for the support I've received over the years from my many friends in the insane and wonderful world that we call "the media biz": Silvie Acevedo, Darrell Ankarlo, Dave Armstrong, Jed Babbin, Don Barrett, Gayle Bass, Barry Besse, Amy Bolton, Steve Bridges, Brenda Vance-Brown, Ernie Brown, Marcus Brown, Tom Brown, Dave Burnett, Greg Burns, Tyler Cox, Blanquita Cullum, Geoff Currier, Mark Davis, Kate Delaney, "Salt and Demetri," Paul Duckworth, Sam Ettaro, Terry Fahy, Vicki Fiorelli, J.D. Freeman, Rich Galen, Mike Gallagher, Jonathan Garthwaite, Kevin Glass, Kevin Godwin, Jim Governale, Stephanie Green, Steve Gregory, Danielle Hampson, Bill Handel, Sean Hannity, Ron Hartenbaum, J.D. Hayworth, Hugh Hewitt, Jeff Hillery, Jimmy Hodson, Geoff Holtzman, Dave Hughes, Rob Hunter, Christine Jones, Kim Ketchel, Jill King, Jerry Klein, John Kodak, Michelle Kube, Michele Larson, Todd Lawley, Justin Levine, Gary Lycan, Jackie Mahaney, Roger Marsh, Kevin Martin, Dawn McCauley, Pat McMahon, Mike Mears, Michael Medved, Kevin Miller, Frank Pastore, Al Peterson, Michael Piercey, Chris Plante, Dave Pratt, Dave Ramsey, Pablo Rios, Robert Robb, Nathalie Rodriguez, Tino Salvaje, Dave Santrella, Ro Scarfo, Robert Schlesinger, Perry Michael Simon, Tyissha Smith, Gregg Stebben, Le Templar, Tom Tradup, Chuck Tyler, Jayme West, Chad Willems, Jason Wilmot, and Barry Young.

AUSTIN HILL

Special thanks to my colleagues in philosophy at Talbot School of Theology for their encouragement of this project, and to my family, who endured a very hectic schedule as I was wrapping up my contribution to this book.

And my thanks to coauthor Austin Hill, who kept insisting that we needed to write this book, and now! Thanks for your partnership and stimulus to complete this project in a timely way.

SCOTT RAE

CITY OF MAN

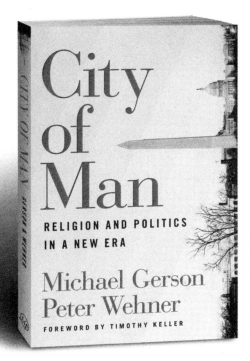

An era has ended. The political expression that most galvanized evangelicals during the past quarter-century, the Religious Right, is fading. What's ahead is unclear. Millions of faith-based voters still exist, and they continue to care deeply about hot-button issues like abortion and same-sex marriage, but the shape of their future political engagement remains to be formed.

Into this uncertainty, former White House insiders Michael Gerson and Peter Wehner seek to call evangelicals toward a new kind of political engage-ment—a kind that is better both for the church and the country, a kind that cannot be co-opted by either political party, a kind that avoids the historic mistakes of both the Religious Left and the Religious Right.

MOODY
PUBLISHERS

www.MoodyPublishers.com

GOOD INTENTIONS

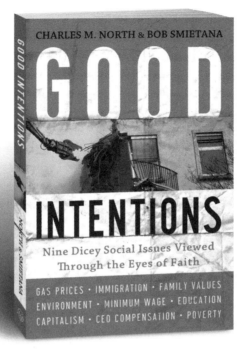

ISBN-13: 978-0-8024-3462-3

Most of us turn to the Bible for decision making, but since the Bible deals in morality and value, it's difficult to apply its principles to the economic choices we make each day. However, by measuring the outcome of these choices with the use of economic theory, we can determine long-range implications and more easily evaluate them according to biblical criteria. *Good Intentions* suggests that it is possible to do good in economic matters if one begins with the right assumptions. By combining a biblical framework with standard economic tools and principles, the authors assess the morality and biblical "rightness" of choices we make every day. Rather than suggesting what readers should think, they provide sound economic reasoning that can be coupled with scriptural directives and examples to help readers make up their own minds about even the thorniest economic issues of our day.

MOODY
PUBLISHERS

www.MoodyPublishers.com